Methods of Authors

by Hugo Erichsen

To

R. E. FRANCILLON,

who is admired and loved by novel-readers on both sides of the Atlantic,

THIS BOOK IS DEDICATED,

by his permission, with sincere regard, by the Author.

PREFACE.

When I began to gather the material for this volume I was quite doubtful as to whether the public would be interested in a work of this kind or not. As my labor progressed, however, it became evident that not only the body of the people, but authors themselves, were deeply interested in the subject, and would welcome a book treating of it. Not only M. Jules Claretie, the celebrated Parisian literarian, but the late Dr. Meissner and many others assured me of this fact.

Nor is this very surprising. Who, after reading a brilliant novel, or some excellent treatise, would not like to know how it was written?

So far as I know, this volume is a novelty, and Ben Akiba is outwitted for once. Books about authors have been published by the thousands, but to my knowledge, up to date, none have been issued describing their methods of work.

In the preparation of this book I have been greatly aided by the works of Rev. Francis Jacox, an anonymous article in All the Year Round, and R. E. Francillon's essay on "The Physiology of Authorship," which appeared first in the Gentleman's Magazine.

I was also assisted in my labor by numerous newspaper clippings and many letters from writers, whose names appear in this volume, and to all of whom I return my sincere thanks.

H. E. DETROIT, Mich.

CONTENTS.

METHODS OF AUTHORS.

I.

Eccentricities in Composition.

The public--that is, the reading world made up of those who love the products of authorship--always takes an interest in the methods of work adopted by literary men, and is fond of gaining information about authorship in the act, and of getting a glimpse of its favorite, the author, at work in that "sanctum sanctorum"--the study. The modes in which men write are so various that it would take at least a dozen volumes to relate them, were they all known, for:--

"Some wits are only in the mind When beaux and belles are 'round them prating; Some, when they dress for dinner, find Their muse and valet both in waiting; And manage, at the self-same time, To adjust a neckcloth and a rhyme.

"Some bards there are who cannot scribble Without a glove to tear or nibble; Or a small twig to whisk about-- As if the hidden founts of fancy, Like wells of old, were thus found out By mystic tricks of rhabdomancy.

"Such was the little feathery wand, That, held forever in the hand Of her who won and wore the crown Of female genius in this age, Seemed the conductor that drew down Those words of lightning to her page."

This refers to Madame, who, when writing, wielded a "little feathery wand," made of paper, shaped like a fan or feather, in the manner and to the effect above described.

Well may the vivacious penman of "Rhymes on the Road" exclaim:--

"What various attitudes, and ways, And tricks we authors have in writing! While some write sitting, some, like Bayes, Usually stand while they're inditing. Poets there are who wear the floor out, Measuring a line at every stride; While some, like Henry Stephens, pour out Rhymes by the dozen while they ride. Herodotus wrote most in bed; And Richerand, a French physician,

Declares the clockwork of the head Goes best in that reclined position. If you consult Montaigne and Pliny on The subject, 'tis their joint opinion That thought its richest harvest yields Abroad, among the woods and fields."

M. de Valois alleges that Plato produced, like Herodotus, "his glorious visions all in bed"; while

"'Twas in his carriage the sublime Sir Richard Blackmore used to rhyme."

But little is known of the habits of the earliest writers. The great Plato, whose thoughts seemed to come so easy, we are told, toiled over his manuscripts, working with slow and tiresome elaboration. The opening sentence of "The Republic" on the author's tablets was found to be written in thirteen different versions. When death called him from his labor the great philosopher was busy at his desk, "combing, and curling, and weaving, and unweaving his writings after a variety of fashions." Virgil was wont to pour forth a quantity of verses in the morning, which he decreased to a very small number by incessant correction and elimination. He subjected the products of his composition to a process of continual polishing and filing, much after the manner, as he said himself, of a bear licking her cubs into shape. Cicero's chief pleasure was literary work. He declared that he would willingly forego all the wealth and glory of the world to spend his time in meditation or study.

The diversity in the methods adopted by authors is as great as the difference in their choice of subjects. A story is often cited in illustration of the different characteristics of three great nationalities which equally illustrates the different paths which may be followed in any intellectual undertaking.

An Englishman, a Frenchman, and a German, competing for a prize offered for the best essay on the natural history of the camel, adopted each his own method of research upon the subject. The German, providing himself with a stock of tobacco, sought the quiet solitude of his study in order to evolve from the depths of his philosophic consciousness the primitive notion of a camel. The Frenchman repaired to the nearest library, and overhauled its contents in order to collect all that other men had written upon the subject. The Englishman packed his carpet-bag and set sail for the East, that he might study the habits of the animal in its original haunts.

The combination of these three methods is the perfection of study; but the Frenchman's method is not unknown even among Americans. Nor does it deserve the condemnation it usually receives. The man who peruses a hundred books on a subject for the purpose of writing one bestows a real benefit upon society, in case he does his work well. But some excellent work has been composed without the necessity either of research or original investigation. Anthony Trollope described his famous archdeacon without ever having met a live archdeacon. He never lived in any cathedral city except London; Archdeacon Grantly was the child of "moral consciousness" alone; Trollope had no knowledge, except indirectly, about bishops and deans. In fact, "The Warden" was not intended originally to be a novel of clerical life, but a novel which should work out a dramatic situation--that of a trustworthy, amiable man who was the holder, by no fault of his own, of an endowment which was in itself an abuse, and on whose devoted head should fall the thunders of those who assailed the abuse.

Bryan Waller Proctor, the poet (who, I believe, is better known under the name of "Barry Cornwall"), had never viewed the ocean when he committed to paper that beautiful poem, "The Sea." Many of his finest lyrics and songs were composed mentally while he was riding daily to London in an omnibus. Schiller had never been in Switzerland, and had only heard and read about the country, when he wrote his "William Tell." Harrison Ainsworth, the Lancashire novelist, when he composed "Rookwood" and "Jack Sheppard," depended entirely on his ability to read up and on his facility of assimilation, for during his lifetime he never came in personal contact with thieves at all. It is said that when he wrote the really admirable ride of Turpin to York he only went at a great pace over the paper, with a road-map and description of the country in front of him. It was only when he heard all the world say how faithfully the region was pictured, and how truly he had observed distances and localities, that he actually drove over the ground for the first time, and declared that it was more like his account than he could have imagined.

Erasmus composed on horseback, as he pricked across the country, and committed his thoughts to paper as soon as he reached his next inn. In this way he composed his "Encomium Mori?" or "Praise of Folly," in a journey from Italy to the land of the man to whose name that title bore punning and complimentary reference, his sterling friend and ally, Sir Thomas More.

Aubrey relates how Hobbes composed his "Leviathan": "He walked much and mused as he walked; and he had in the head of his cane a pen and inkhorn, and he carried always a note-book in his pocket, and 'as soon as the thought darted,' he presently entered it into his book, or otherwise might have lost it. He had drawn the design of the book into chapters, etc., and he knew whereabouts it would come in." Hartley Coleridge somewhere expresses his entire conviction that it was Pope's general practice to set down in a book every line, half-line, or lucky phrase that occurred to him, and either to find or make a place for them when and where he could. Richard Savage noted down a whole tragedy on scraps of paper at the counters of shops, into which he entered and asked for pen and ink as if to make a memorandum.

"A man would do well to carry a pencil in his pocket, and write down the thoughts of the moment. Those that come unsought are generally the most valuable, and should be secured, because they seldom return." This was the advice of Lord Bacon, whose example has been followed by many eminent men. Miss Martineau has recorded that Barry Cornwall's favorite method of composition was practised when alone in a crowd. He, like Savage, also had a habit of running into a shop to write down his verses. Tom Moore's custom was to compose as he walked. He had a table in his garden, on which he wrote down his thoughts. When the weather was bad, he paced up and down his small study. It is extremely desirable that thoughts should be written as they rise in the mind, because, if they are not recorded at the time, they may never return. "I attach so much importance to the ideas which come during the night, or in the morning," says Gaston Plante, the electrical engineer, "that I have always, at the head of my bed, paper and pencil suspended by a string, by the help of which I write every morning the ideas I have been able to conceive, particularly upon subjects of scientific research. I write these notes in obscurity, and decipher and develop them in the morning, pen in hand." The philosopher Emerson took similar pains to catch a fleeting thought, for, whenever he had a happy idea, he wrote it down, and when Mrs. Emerson, startled in the night by some unusual sound, cried, "What is the matter? Are you ill?" the philosopher softly replied, "No, my dear; only an idea."

George Bancroft, the historian, had a similar habit. His bedroom served also as a library. The room was spacious, and its walls were lined, above and below, with volumes. A single bed stood in the middle of the apartment, and beside the bed were paper, pencil, two wax candles, and matches; so that, like Mr. Pecksniff, Mr. Bancroft might not forget any idea that came into his mind in a wakeful moment of the night.

As curious a mode of composition as perhaps any on record, if the story be credible, is that affirmed of Fuller--that he used to write the first words of every line near the margin down to the foot of the paper, and that then, beginning again, he filled up the blanks exactly, without spaces, interlineations, or contractions, and that he would so connect the ends and beginnings that the sense would appear as complete as if it had been written in a continued series after the ordinary manner.

Several distinguished American writers have the habit of jotting a sentence, or a line or two here and there, upon a long page, and then filling up the outline thus made with persistent revision.

With some great writers, it has been customary to do a vast amount of antecedent work before beginning their books. It is related of George Eliot that she read one thousand books before she wrote "Daniel Deronda." For two or three years before she composed a work, she read up her subject in scores and scores of volumes. She was one of the masters, so called, of all learning, talking with scholars and men of science on terms of equality. George Eliot was a hard worker, and, like many gifted writers, she was often tempted to burn at night the lines she had written during the day. Carlyle was similarly tempted, and it is to be regretted that the great growler, in many instances, did not carry out the design. Carlyle spent fifteen years on his "Frederick the Great." Alison perused two thousand books before he completed his celebrated history. It is said of another that he read twenty thousand volumes and wrote only two books. "For the statistics of the negro population of South America alone," says Robert Dale Owen, "I examined more than 150 volumes." David Livingstone said: "Those who have never carried a book through the press can form no idea of the amount of toil it involves. The process has increased my respect for authors a thousandfold. I think I would rather cross the African continent again than to undertake to write another book."

Thackeray confessed that the title for his novel, "Vanity Fair," came to him in the middle of the night, and that he jumped out of bed and ran three times around the room, shouting the words. Thackeray had no literary system. He wrote only when he felt like it. Sometimes he was unable to write two lines in succession. Then, again, he could sit down and write so rapidly that he would keep three sheets in the wind all the time. While he was editor of the Cornhill Magazine he never succeeded in getting copy enough ahead for more than five issues. In this negligence he fell far behind the magazine editors of the present time. They always have bundles of copy on hand.

II.

Care in Literary Production.

Indolence, that is to say, chronic fatigue, appears to be the natural habit of imaginative brains. It is a commonplace to note that men of fertile fancy, as a class, have been notorious for their horror of formulating their ideas even by the toil of thought, much more by passing them through the crucible of the ink-bottle. In many cases they have needed the very active stimulant of hunger. The caco 齳 hes scribendi is a disease common, not to imaginative, but to imitative, minds. Probably no hewer of wood or drawer of water undergoes a tithe of the toil of those whose work is reputed play, but is, in fact, a battle, every moment, between the flesh and the spirit. Campbell, who at the age of sixty-one could drudge at an unimaginative work for fourteen hours a day like a galley-slave, "and yet," as he says in one of his letters, "be as cheerful as a child," speaks in a much less happy tone of the work which alone was congenial to him: "The truth is, I am not writing poetry, but projecting it, and that keeps me more idle and abstracted than you can conceive. I pass hours thinking about what I am to compose. The actual time employed in composition is but a fraction of the time lost in setting about it." "At Glasgow," we read of him even when a young man, "he seldom exercised his gift except when roused into action either by the prospect of gaining a prize or by some striking incident." Campbell, if not a great man, was a typical worker.

A playwright, who had written five hundred lines in three days, taunted Euripides because he had spent as much time upon five lines. "Yes," replied the poet, "but your five hundred lines in three days will be forgotten, while my five will live forever."

It is said of one of Longfellow's poems that it was written in four weeks, but that he spent six months in correcting and cutting it down. Longfellow was a very careful writer. He wrote and rewrote, and laid his work by and later revised it. He often consulted his friends about his productions before they were given to the world. Thus he sent his work out as perfect as great care and a brilliant intellect could make it. The poet's pleasant surroundings must have acted as a stimulus upon his mind. His library was a long room in the northeastern corner of the lower floor in the so-called Craigie House, once the residence of General Washington. It was walled with handsome bookcases, rich in choice works. The poet's usual seat here was at a little high table by the north window, looking upon the garden. Some of his work was done while he was standing at this table, which reached then to his breast.

Emerson wrote with great care, and would not only revise his manuscript carefully, but frequently rewrite the article upon the proof-sheets.

John Owen was twenty years on his "Commentary on the Epistle of the Hebrews."

The celebrated French critic, Sainte-Beuve, was accustomed to devote six days to the preparation of a single one of his weekly articles. A large portion of his time was passed in the retirement of his chamber, to which, on such occasions, no one--with the exception of his favorite servant--was allowed to enter under any circumstances whatever. Here he wrote those critical papers which carried captive the heart of France, and filled with wonder cultivated minds everywhere.

The historian Gibbon, in speaking of the manner in which he wrote his "Decline and Fall of the Roman Empire," said: "Many experiments were made before I could hit the middle tone between a dull tone and a rhetorical declamation. Three times did I compose the first chapter, and twice the second and third, before I was tolerably satisfied with their effect." Gibbon spent twenty years on his immortal book Lamb toiled most laboriously over his essays. These papers, which long ago took their place in the English classical language and which are replete with the most delicate fancies, were composed with the most exacting nicety, yet their author is regarded the world over as possessed of genius of a high order.

La Rochefoucauld was occupied for the space of fifteen years in preparing for publication his little work called "Maximes," rewriting many of them more than thirty times.

Honor?de Balzac had just completed his teens when he arrived in Paris, and till 1830, some nine years, he lived, not in a garret, but in the apartment over that, called a grenier; his daily expenses amounted to about half a franc-- three sous for bread, three for milk, and the rest for firewood and candles. He passed his days in the public library of the Arsenal, devouring books. In the evening he transcribed his notes, and during the nights he took his walks abroad, and so gained an insight into the depths of human depravity.

After his first novel, in 1830, he commenced earning money. Balzac, who had the disease of creative genius in its most outrageous form, "preached to us," says Theophile Gautier, "the strangest hygiene ever propounded among laymen. If we desired to hand our names down to posterity as authors, it was indispensable that we should immure ourselves absolutely for two or three years; that we should drink nothing but water, and eat only soaked beans, like Protogenes; that we should go to bed at sunset and rise at midnight, to work hard till morning; that we should spend the whole day in revising, amending, extending, pruning, perfecting, and polishing our night's work, in correcting proofs or taking notes, or in other necessary study." If the author happened to be in love, he was to see the lady of his heart only for one half-hour a year, but he might write to her, for the cold-blooded reason that letter-writing improves the style. Not only did Balzac preach this austere doctrine, but he practised it as nearly as he could without ceasing altogether to be a man and a Frenchman. Gozlan's account of the daily life of the author of the "Commie Humaine" has often been quoted. On the average he worked eighteen hours a day. He began his day with dinner at six in the afternoon, at which, while he fed his friends generously, he himself ate little besides fruit and drank nothing but water. At seven o'clock he wished his friends good-night, and went to bed. At midnight he rose and worked--till dinner-time next day: and so the world went round. George Sand calls him, "Drunk on water, intemperate in work, and sober in all other passions." Jules Janin asks, "Where has M. de Balzac gained his knowledge of woman--he, the anchorite?" As it was, love and death came to him hand-in-hand. He married a wealthy Polish lady in 1848. They travelled over the battlefields of Europe, to collect notes for a work, and then settled down in a luxurious mansion in the Champs Elysees. Nothing was wanting in that palatial residence, for every fancy of Balzac had been gratified. Three months after the house-warming Balzac was dead.

Balzac, after he had made a plan of a novel, and had, after the most laborious research, gathered together the materials which he was to embody in it, locked himself in his private apartment, shut out all the light of day, and then, by the aid of his study lamp, he toiled day and night. His servants, knowing so well his peculiar habits, brought him food and drink. Finally, with his task completed, as he thought, he came forth from his retirement looking more dead than alive. But invariably his task was not altogether satisfactory to him, after all, for again he would seek the seclusion of his chamber to rearrange and make more perfect that which he had before supposed wholly complete. Then, too, when his work was in the hands of the printer, he was as apt as not to alter, in one way and another, the manuscript, until both printer and publisher were on the verge of despair. He corrected up to as many as twelve proofs, and many of his "corrections" consisted in rewriting whole pages. What "copy" he must have produced during the twenty years in which he brought out ninety-seven volumes! Like Voltaire, Balzac had a passion for coffee, more to keep him awake than as a stimulant. That beverage shortened his life, which ended by hypertrophy of the heart. When he sat down to his desk, his servant, who regarded a man that abstained even from tobacco as scarcely human, used to place coffee within reach, and upon this he worked till his full brain would drive his starved and almost sleepless body into such forgetfulness that he often found himself at daybreak bareheaded, in dressing gown and slippers, in the Place du Carrousel, not knowing how he came there, miles away from home. Now, coffee acts upon some temperaments as laudanum acts upon others, and many of the manners and customs of Balzac were those of a confirmed opium-eater. He had the same strange illusions, the same extravagant ideas, the same incapacity for distinguishing with regard to outward things, between the possible and the impossible, the false and the true. His midnight wanderings, his facility in projecting himself into personalities utterly unlike his own, belong to the experiences of the "English Opium-eater."

Kinglake's beautiful "Eothen" was rewritten half a dozen times before it was given to a publisher.

Tennyson's song, "Come Into the Garden, Maud," was rewritten some fifty times before it gave complete satisfaction to the author.

Coming to the gifted Addison, whose diction is full of such grace and simplicity, so much so as to create envy, yet admiration, in the mind of every writer who has flourished since his day, we find that the great author wrote with the most painful deliberation. It is narrated that the press was stopped again and again, after a whole edition of the Spectator had been thrown off, in order that its author might make a slight change in a sentence.

Tom Moore, with all his wonderful brilliancy, considered it doing very well if he wrote fifty lines of his "Lalla Rookh" in a week.

Hawthorne was slow in composing. Sometimes he wrote only what amounted to half a dozen pages a week, often only a few lines in the same space of time, and, alas! he frequently went to his chamber and took up his pen, only to find himself wholly unable to perform any literary work.

The author of "Pleasures of Hope" was slow of thought, and consequently his mode of composition was toilsome in the highest degree. He wrote with extreme caution, weighing and shaping the effect of each particular line before he permitted it to stand.

Bret Harte, whose creations read as if they had come from his brain without a flaw or hindrance, showing brilliancy of thought with the grace of the artist, is still another writer who passes days and weeks on a short story or poem before he is ready to deliver it into the hands of the printer. So it was with Bryant. Though in reality the sum total of his poetry might be included in a small volume, so few are his lyrics, we cannot fail to be impressed with the truth of the statement when we are told that even these few gems of verse cost our late Wordsworth hard toil to bring into being, and endow with the splendor of immortality.

Bernardine de St. Pierre copied his sweet and beautiful "Paul and Virginia" nine times to make it more perfect.

B 閞 anger composait toutes ses chansons dans sa te. "Once made, I committed them to writing in order to forget them," he said. He tells of having dreamt for ten years of a song about the taxes that weigh down the rural population. In vain he tapped his brain-pan,--nothing came of it. But one night he awoke with the air and the refrain tout trouv 閺:

"Jacques, le-toi; Voici venir l'huissier du roi";

and in a day or two the song was a made thing.

The laborious pains bestowed by Alfieri on the process of composition may seem at first sight hard to reconcile with his impulsive character. If he approved his first sketch of a piece,--after laying it by for some time, not approaching it again until his mind was free of the subject,--he submitted it to what he called "development," i. e., writing out in prose the indicated scenes, with all the force at his command, but without stopping to analyze a thought or correct an expression. "He then proceeded to versify at his leisure the prose he had written, selecting with care the ideas he thought best, and rejecting those which he deemed" unworthy of a place. Nor did he ever yet regard this work as finished, but "incessantly polished it verse by verse and made continual alterations," as might seem to him expedient.

Hartley Coleridge so far resembled Alfieri that it was his custom to put aside what he had written for some months, till the heat and excitement of composition had effervesced, and then he thought it was in a fair condition to criticise. But he seldom altered. "Strike the nail on the anvil," was his advice; he never "kneaded or pounded" his thoughts, which have been described as always coming out cap-?pie, like a troop in quick march. He used to brandish his pen in the act of composition, now and then beating time with his foot, and breaking out into a shout at any felicitous idea.

III.

Speed in Writing.

Dr. Johnson was a very rapid writer. A modern critic says of him: "He had but to dip his pen in ink, and there flowed out a current of thought and language wide and voluminous as the Ganges in flood." Some of the best papers in the Rambler were written "currente calamo." Johnson struck off his Ramblers and Idlers at a heat when the summons of the press forbade his indolence to put off his work another moment: he did not give himself even a minute to read over his papers before they went to the printers. Often he sent a portion of the copy of an essay, and wrote the remainder while the earlier part was printing. His "Life of Savage" was dashed off at one sitting. Sir Joshua Reynolds was so fascinated with this eloquent and touching narrative, that he could not lay it down until he had finished it. Johnson would not have written "Rasselas" except for the necessity of paying the costs of his mother's funeral. He was an extremely indolent man, and yet he was a laborious worker where the imagination was not concerned. After spending the evening at the literary club in the society of Burke, Goldsmith, and other friends, he returned home between midnight and sunrise, went to bed, and was seldom seen before noon. Bennet Langton was so delighted with the Rambler, that he went to London to be introduced to Johnson. He called upon him about twelve o'clock, but the great doctor was not yet visible. After waiting some time, the author of the Rambler made his appearance. The visitor expected to see a neatly dressed philosopher, but, instead, a huge, uncouth figure rolled into the room in a soiled morning-gown, with an ill-arranged wig, and stockings falling over his shoes.

The elder Dumas, in order to get any work done at all, had to forbid himself, by an effort of will, to leave his desk before a certain number of pages were written. Victor Hugo is said to have locked up his clothes while writing "Notre-Dame," so that he might not escape from it till the last word was written. In such cases the so-called "pleasures of imagination" look singularly like the pains of stone-breaking. The hardest part of the lot of genius, we suspect, has been not the emotional troubles popularly--and with absurd exaggeration--ascribed to it, but a disgust for labor during the activity of the fancy, and the necessity for labor when it is most disgusting.

Victor Hugo composed with wonderful rapidity. He wrote his "Cromwell" in three months, and his "Notre Dame de Paris" in four months and a half. But even these have been his longest periods of labor, and as he grew older he wrote faster. "Marion Delorme" was finished in twenty-four days, "Hernani" in twenty-six, and "Le Roi s'amuse" in twenty. Although the poet wrote very quickly, he often corrected laboriously. He rarely rewrote. Mme. Drouet, who was his literary secretary for thirty years, copied all his manuscripts.

Otherwise the printers would have found him one of the most difficult authors to put into type. Mme. Drouet saved them much worry, and himself or his publishers much expense in the way of composition. She also assisted in the correction of the proofs. He generally had several works in the stocks at the same time. Hugo considered a change of subject a recreation. He would go from poetry to fiction, from fiction to history, according to his mood. As a rule, he rose at six o'clock in the morning, took a cold bath, then took a raw egg and a cup of black coffee, and went to work. He never sat down to write, but stood at a high desk, and refreshed himself by an occasional turn across the room, and a sip of eau sucr 閑. He breakfasted at eleven. One of his recreations was riding on the top of an omnibus, a habit he contracted during a short visit to London, when he was advised that "the knife-board" was a good place from which to see the street life of the English metropolis. The "knife-board," indeed, was his favorite point of observation, whence he gathered inspiration from the passing crowds below. Many of his famous characters have been caught in his mind's eye while taking a three-sou drive from the Arc de Triomphe to the Bastile.

It is on record that Bulwer wrote his romance of "Harold" in less than a month, resting not at all by day, and scarcely at night. In a private letter Lord Lytton says: "The novel of 'Harold' was written in rather less than four weeks. I can personally attest this fact, as I was with my father when he wrote it--on a visit to his friend, the late Mr. Tennyson D'Eyncourt. D'Eyncourt was a great collector of Norman and Anglo-Saxon chronicles, with which his library was well stored. The notes of research for 'Harold' fill several thick commonplace books.... While my father was writing 'Harold' I do not think he put down his pen except for meals and half an hour's run before dinner 'round the terrace. He was at work the greater part of every night, and again early in the morning."

It is an interesting fact in regard to Lord Tennyson's drama on the same subject--with a dedication to the late Lord Lytton, in reconciliation of an old literary feud with his father--that the first sketch of "Harold" took the form of a drama, entitled "William the Norman." It was probably not written for publication, as the writer's way of composing many of his prose romances was to sketch them out first as dramas.

The "Lady of Lyons" was written in ten days. It was by no means uncommon with Bulwer to have two books in hand at once, and live alternate periods with the beings of his creation, as if he were passing in society from one company to another. Thus "Lucretia" and "The Caxtons," "Kenelm Chillingly" and "The Parisians," were written simultaneously. But despite his literary facility, Bulwer rewrote some of his briefer productions as many as eight or nine times before their publication. Another author tells us that he wrote paragraphs and whole pages of his book as many as fifty times.

Byron wrote the "Bride of Abydos" in a single night, and the quill pen with which he performed this marvellous feat is still preserved in the British Museum.

Dryden wrote "Alexander's Feast" in two days.

"The Merry Wives of Windsor" was composed in a fortnight.

Beckford finished "Vathek" in two days and nights.

Henry Ward Beecher's publishers have favored the world with an account of his habits in composition. "He wrote," they tell us, "with inconceivable rapidity, in a large, sprawling hand, lines wide apart, and words so thinly scattered about that some of the pages remind one of the famous description of a page of Napoleon's manuscript--a scratch, a blot, and a splutter." This is, indeed, remarkable, but is far exceeded by the performance in that line of a famous Chinese novelist, who wrote with such fearful speed, that, throwing the finished sheets over his head, they soon accumulated to a pile large enough to darken his windows, and threaten him with suffocation.

Horace, in one of his satires, makes fun of a contemporary poet, whose chief claim to distinction was that he could compose two hundred verses standing on one leg. Horace did not think much of the verses, and, we suspect with good reason.

There are all conceivable habits of composition, and they range from the slow elaboration of John Foster to the race-horse speed of our doughty Southern countryman, Henry A. Wise, whose prodigious gubernatorial compositions are still remembered by a suffering world. Once, sitting by James Parton, he observed, tersely, "The best writing distils from the pen drop by drop." Sheridan once said to a friend who had a fatal facility with his pen, "Your easy writing makes terribly hard reading."

I would not, for the world, have the young men of the country believe that in writing speed is all. One should not be ambitious to write or do anything else any faster than he can do it well. It was Henry Wadsworth Longfellow who once gave this excellent advice to a young author: "Always write your best; remember, your best."

Wilkie Collins' book, "Heart and Science," so mercilessly excited him that he says he continued writing week after week without a day's interval or rest. "Rest was impossible. I made a desperate effort; rushed to the sea; went sailing and fishing, and was writing my book all the time 'in my head,' as the children say. The one wise course to take was to go back to my desk and empty my head, and then rest. My nerves are too much shaken for travelling. An armchair and a cigar, and a hundred and fiftieth reading of the glorious Walter Scott,--King, Emperor, and President of Novelists,--there is the regimen that is doing me good. All the other novel-writers I can read while I am at work myself. If I only look at the 'Antiquary' or 'Old Mortality,' I am crushed by the sense of my own littleness, and there is no work possible for me on that day."

Wilkie Collins made the skeleton of a novel and then proceeded to put the flesh on it. He was the greatest plotter that ever lived. He created no truly great characters, but his stories are full of thrilling pitfalls, into which the reader lunges.

Hugo Rosenthal-Bonin, the editor of Ueber Land und Meer (one of the most prominent of the illustrated journals of Germany), and the author of many successful novels, writes for two hours immediately after breakfast and dinner, and within this time regularly composes five columns of reading matter, never rewriting a single line. While writing, he has a piece of looking-glass lying beside him, the glittering of which (so he says) stimulates and refreshes him; he also smokes cigars during working hours, otherwise seldom. He works with ease and rapidity, just as if he were speaking. Therefore, a novel of ten columns is finished within two days, and a romance of one hundred columns is completed in less than a month. He has never written more than one long novel a year, his literary productiveness being limited by his duties as editor.

Mrs. Helen Hunt Jackson ("H. H.") composed with great rapidity, writing on large sheets of yellow post-office paper, eschewing pen and ink, and insisting that a lead pencil alone could keep pace with the swiftness of her thoughts.

Emil Ritterhaus, the poet who "dwells by the castled Rhine," turns out lyrical poems without any difficulty, and with wonderful rapidity. That poem of his which was read at the consecration of the cathedral at Cologne was composed in a few minutes, in the presence of his friend, Ferdinand Hiller, not a line being changed afterward. When he is in the proper mood, many a speech of his turns involuntarily into an improvisation. Verses he pens in person, but he dictates all other literary work. When at work, a good Havana cigar, a glass of first-class wine, or a cup of strong coffee are agreeable to him. When dictating, he is in the habit of lying on a sofa or walking slowly up and down the room. The poet makes it a rule not to write unless disposed to.

Gray found fault with Mason for fancying he should succeed best by writing hastily in the first fervors of his imaginations, and, therefore, never waiting for epithets if they did not occur at the time readily, but leaving spaces for them, and putting them in afterward. This enervated his poetry, said Gray, and he says the same thing of the same method by whomsoever adopted, for nothing is done so well as at the first concoction. One of Shelley's biographers came upon the poet in a pine forest, writing verses on a guitar, and, picking up a fragment, saw a "frightful scrawl," all smear, and smudge, and disorder-- such a dashed-off daub as conceited artists are apt to mistake for genius. Shelley said: "When my brain gets heated with thought, it soon boils, and throws off images and words faster than I can skim them off. In the morning, when cooled down, out of that rude sketch, as you justly call it, I shall attempt a drawing."

IV.

Influence upon Writers of Time and Place.

Nathaniel Hawthorne made innumerable notes of every fleeting, quaint fancy, strange anecdote, or eccentric person. These notes he afterward worked into his stories. Julian Hawthorne, his son, states in the Century

Magazine: "The new husband and wife, Adam and Eve, as they liked to call themselves, were almost as poor in money as their prototypes, and in spite of their orchard and their vegetable garden, a good deal less able to get on without occasional remittances. Accordingly, the future author of the 'Scarlet Letter' was compelled to alternate his hoeing and digging, his rambles over the hills and his paddling on the river, with periods of application to pen and paper in his study, where he would sit with locked doors, clad in a long and ancient flowered dressing-gown, upon the lining of the left-hand skirt of which he was in the habit of wiping his pen. His wife noticed this habit, and said nothing about it; but one day, on bringing his pen to the accustomed spot, Hawthorne found stitched on there a pretty pen-wiper, in the shape of a butterfly with red and black wings, and this butterfly was ever after renewed from time to time, as necessity required. What was written in that little sunny-hued study, readers know, but nobody, not even the author's wife, ever saw him in the act of writing. He had to be alone."

Burns usually composed while walking in the open air, influenced, perhaps, Dr. Currie suggests, by habits formed in early life. Until he was completely master of a tune, he never could write words for it; so his way was to consider the poetic sentiment corresponding to his idea of the musical expression; then choose his theme; begin one stanza; when that was composed,--which was generally the most difficult part of the task,--to walk out, sit down now and then, look out for objects in nature around him, such as harmonized with the cogitations of his fancy, humming occasionally the air, with the verses already framed. When he felt his "muse beginning to jade," he retired to the solitary fireside of his study, and there committed his thoughts to paper; swinging at intervals on the hind leg of his elbow-chair, "by way," he says, "of calling forth my own critical strictures as my pen goes on." Sometimes, and more than once too often, he composed, to use his own expression, "by the leeside of a bowl of punch, which had overset every mortal in company, except the hautbois and the muse."

Whether in town or country, Landor reflected and composed habitually while walking, and, therefore, preferred at all times to walk alone. So did Buckle. Wordsworth was accustomed to compose his verse in his solitary walks, carry it in his memory, and get wife or daughter to write it down on his return. He used to compose aloud while walking in the fields and woods. Sometimes he would use a slate pencil and the smooth side of a rock to jot down his lines. His excursions and peculiar habits gave rise to some anxious beliefs among the ignorant peasantry. Even his sanity was questioned. The peasantry of Rydal thought him "not quite hissel," because he always walked alone, and was met at odd times in odd places. Some poets have been in the habit of humming or repeating their verses aloud as they composed them. Southey, for instance, boomed his verses so as to be mistaken by Wilson, who was a keen sportsman, for a bittern booming. If this is true, Southey's voice must not have been very harmonious, for the bittern's cry is Shakespeare's "night-raven's dismal voice."

Douglas Jerrold worked at a desk without a speck upon it, using an ink-stand in a marble shell clear of all litter, his little dog at his feet. If a comedy was in progress, he would now and then walk rapidly up and down the room, talking wildly to himself. "If it be Punch copy, you shall hear him laugh presently as he hits upon a droll bit." And then, abruptly, the pen would be put down, and the author would pass out into the garden, and pluck a hawthorn leaf, and go, nibbling it and thinking, down the side walks; then "in again, and vehemently to work," unrolling the thought that had come to him along little blue slips of paper, in letters smaller than the type in which they were presently to be set.

Dr. Channing had the same habit of taking a turn in the garden, during which he was a study for the calm concentration of his look, and the deliberateness of his step: "Calmer, brighter, in a few moments he is seated again at his table, and his rapidly flying pen shows how full is the current of his thoughts."

Jane Taylor, who commenced authorship as a very little girl indeed, and who used at that early stage to compose tales and dramas while whipping a top,--committing them to paper at the close of that exercise,--was in the habit, her brother Isaac tells us, of rambling for half an hour after breakfast, "to seek that pitch of excitement without which she never took up the pen."

Of Dickens we are told that "some quaint little bronze figures on his desk were as much needed for the easy flow of his writing as blue ink or quill pens."

Emanuel Kant, the philosopher, lived the life of a student; in fact, his life may be taken as the type of that of a scholar. Kant, like Balzac, gave a daily dinner-party; but when his guests were gone he took a walk in the country instead of seeking broken slumbers in a state of hunger. He came home at twilight, and read from candle-light till bedtime at ten. He arose punctually at five, and, over one cup of tea and part of a pipe, laid out his plan of work for the day. At seven he lectured, and wrote till dinner-time at about one. The regularity of his life was automatic. He regulated his diet with the care of a physician. During the blind-man's holiday between his walk and candle-light he sat down to think in twilight fashion; and while thus engaged, he always placed himself so that his eyes might fall on a certain old tower. This old tower became so necessary to his thoughts that, when some poplar trees grew up and hid it from his sight, he found himself unable to think at all, until, at his earnest request, the trees were cropped and the tower was brought into sight again.

Kant's old tower recalls Buffon's incapability of thinking to good purpose except in full dress, and with his hair in such elaborate order that, by way of external stimulus to his brain, he had a hairdresser to interrupt his work twice, or, when very busy, thrice a day. To Aubrey we owe this account of Prynne's method of study: "He wore a long quilt cap, which came two or three inches at least over his eyes, and served him as an umbrella to defend his eyes from the light. About every three hours his man was to bring him a roll and a pot of ale, to refocillate his wasted spirits; so he studied and drank and munched some bread; and this maintained him till night, and then he made a good supper." Refocillation is a favorite resource--whatever the word may be--with authors not a few. Addison, with his bottle of wine at each end of the long gallery at Holland House,--and Schiller, with his flask of old Rhenish and his coffee laced with old Cognac, at three in the morning,--occur to the memory at once. Shelley attempted to ruin his digestion by way of exciting the brain by continually munching bread while composing.

The venerable Leopold von Ranke, one of the most eminent historians of the age, composed in the night as well as in the daytime, and even when more than ninety years of age sometimes worked till midnight. He had two secretaries. He was a late riser, as most night-workers are. After getting up late, he worked with his first amanuensis from ten in the morning until three in the afternoon. Thereupon, if the weather was fine, he took a walk in the public promenades, always accompanied by a servant. He dined at five P. M., and then dictated to his second secretary from six in the evening until, occasionally, one or two o'clock in the morning. He neither took stimulants nor smoked. He never worked when disinclined; in fact, the disinclination to write was foreign to his nature. He always felt like writing.

J. T. Trowbridge, the author of "The Vagabonds," always prefers daytime to night for literary work, but sometimes can compose verse only at night. He always sets out with a tolerably distinct outline in his mind--rarely on paper-- of what he intends to write. But the filling in he leaves to the suggestions of thought in the hour of composition, and often gets on to currents which carry him into unexpected by-ways. He seldom begins a story that he would not like to make twice as long as his contract allows, so many incidents and combinations suggest themselves as he goes on. He never works under the influence of stimulants. Verse he never composes with a pen in his hand. It is seldom that he can compose any that is in the least satisfactory to himself; when he can, he walks in pleasant places, if the weather is favorable, or lounges on rocks or banks, or in the woods; or he lies on a sofa in a dimly-lighted room at night; or in bed, where he elaborates his lines, which he retains in his memory, to be written down at the first convenient season. He rarely puts pen to paper at night. When fairly launched in a prose composition, he writes from two to four hours a day, seldom five. The mere act of writing is a sad drudgery to him, and he often has to force himself to begin. Then he usually forgets the drudgery in the interest excited by the development of his thoughts. But he never thinks it wise to continue writing when he cannot do so with pleasure and ease. In his younger days he used to think he must do a certain amount of work each day, whether he felt like it or not. But now he is of the opinion that it might have been better for his readers and himself if he had been governed more by his moods.

Robert Hamerling, the Austrian novelist, loved to compose in bed in the early hours of morning. He was an expert stenographer, and, therefore, made use of stenography when committing his thoughts to paper, thereby saving much time, which, of course, facilitated the mental labor. For this reason, he could also correct and improve the manuscript, as well as make additions to the same, with the least waste of time. He did not require refreshments at work, and wrote with remarkable facility. The duration of the time which he spent at the writing-desk depended upon the state of his health and the temper of his mind.

Frederick Friedrich, well known in Germany as a novelist, prefers the evening for literary work, although he conceives the plots of his stories in the course of the day. He asserts that the nerves are more stimulated and that the imagination is more lively in the evening. His novels are sent to the printer as they were written; he hardly ever makes corrections. While at work Friedrich fills the air with cigar smoke and drinks several glasses of Rhine-wine. He must be alone, and the writing-table must be in the customary order; any new arrangement of the things on the table makes the author feel uncomfortable, so much so at times that it prevents him from writing. He is a facile writer, and composes with great speed. He never writes unless inclined to, and is governed by moods. Therefore, a week or two sometimes passes before he pens a line, being in perfect health, but lacking the inclination to perform intellectual work. He never devotes more than three hours a day to literary labor, generally less than that, but spends almost all day in thinking over the plots of his novels. He never begins a story until it is elaborated in his mind, and never makes notes. When once engaged in the composition of a novel, he keeps at it day after day until it is finished. While writing his own he is unable to read the novels of anybody else.

Celia Thaxter evolves her graceful verses in the daytime. She sometimes makes a skeleton of her work first, not always; and very often forces herself to work in spite of disinclination.

The Austrian poet, Rudolph Baumbach, is partial to daylight, and never writes at night. He always makes an outline of his work before beginning in good earnest. When meditating on his poems he walks up and down the room, but gives the open air the preference. He likes much light; when the sun does not shine his work does not progress favorably. In the evening he lights up his room by a large number of candles. Literary labor is pleasure to him when the weather is fine, but it is extremely hard when clouds shut out the sunlight. The poet has no fixed rule as regards working-hours; sometimes he exerts himself a great deal for weeks, and then again he does not write at all for a long time.

Otto von Leixner, German historian, poet, novelist, and essayist, composes prose, which requires logical thinking, in the daytime, but does poetical work, which taxes principally the imagination, in the evening. He makes a skeleton of all critical and scientific compositions, indeed of all essays, and then writes out the "copy" for the press, seldom making alterations. But he files away at poems from time to time until he thinks them fit for publication. He is a smoker, but does not smoke when at work. Whether promenading the shady walks of a wood or perambulating the dusty streets of the city, Leixner constantly thinks about the works he has in hand. Literary work has no difficulties for this author; he penned one of his poems, "The Vision," consisting of five hundred and eighty lines, in three hours and a half and sent it to the printer as it was originally written; and he composed the novel "Adja," thirty-nine and one-half octavo pages in print, in nine hours. But he often meditates over the topics which go to make up his novels, etc., for years and years until he has considered them from every standpoint. After composition he often locks up his manuscript in his desk for half a year, until it is almost forgotten, when he takes it from its place of concealment and examines it carefully to detect possible errors. If at such an examination the work does not prove satisfactory to him, he throws it into the stove. Being the editor of a journal of fiction, he is often compelled to work whether he wants to or not. From 1869 to 1870 he worked sixteen hours a day; from 1877 till 1882 about thirteen hours, even Sundays; at present he spends from ten to eleven hours every day at the writing-table, unless kept from work by visitors. He retains his health by taking a daily walk, rain or shine, to which he devotes two hours. Leixner lives a very temperate life and hardly ever imbibes stimulating drinks.

The greatest of all Southern poets, Paul Hamilton Hayne, had no particular time for composition, writing as often in the daytime as at night. Whether he made an outline or skeleton of his work first, depended upon the nature of the poem. When the piece was elaborate, he outlined it, and subsequently filled up, much as a painter would do. The poet used to smoke a great deal in composing, but was obliged to abandon tobacco, having had attacks of hemorrhage. He used tea instead of coffee sometimes, but took little even of that. Wine he did not use. Hayne composed best when walking, or riding upon horseback, and as he was seldom without a book in hand, wrote a great deal on the fly-leaves of any volume he chanced to be consulting. He frequently had to force himself to work when he did not have an inclination to do so.

V.

Writing under Difficulties.

It is an exceptional mind that enables an author to write at his ease amid interruptions and distractions, lets and hindrances, of a domestic kind. H 闹 oise gave this singular reason for her constant refusal to become Abelard's wife--that no mind devoted to the meditations of philosophy could endure the cries of children, the chatter of nurses, and the babble and coming and going in and out of serving men and women. Of Abelard himself, however, we are told that he had a rare power of abstracting himself from all outward concerns; that no one knew better how to be alone, though surrounded by others; and that, in fact, his senses took no note of outward things. When Cumberland was composing any work, he never shut himself up in his study, but always wrote in the room where his family sat, and did not feel in the least disturbed by the noise of his children at play beside him. The literary habits of Lord Hailes, as Mr. Robert Chambers remarks, were hardly such as would have been expected from his extreme nicety of diction: it was in no secluded sanctum, or "den," that he composed, but by the "parlour fireside," with wife and bairns within very present sight and sound.

Cowper describes himself at Weston (1791) as working in a study exposed to all manner of inroads, and in no way disconcerted by the coming and going of servants, or other incidental and inevitable impediments. A year or two later he writes from the same spot, "amidst a chaos of interruptions," including Hayley spouting Greek, and Mrs. Unwin talking sometimes to them, sometimes to herself. Francis Horner relates a visit he and a friend paid to Jeremy Bentham at Ford Abbey, one spacious room in which, a tapestried chamber, the utilitarian philosopher had utilized for what he called his "scribbling shop"--two or three tables being set out, covered with white napkins, on which were placed music desks with manuscripts; and here the visitors were allowed to be "present at the mysteries, for he went on as if we had not been with him."

The fourth of Dr. Chalmers' Astronomical Discourses was penned in a small pocket-book, in a strange apartment, where he was liable every moment to interruption; for it was at the manse of Balmerino, disappointed in not finding the minister at home, and having a couple of hours to spare,--and in a drawing-room at the manse of Kilmany, with all the excitement of meeting for the first time, after a year's absence, many of his former friends and parishioners,--that he penned paragraph after paragraph of a composition which, as his son-in-law and biographer, Dr. Hanna, says, bears upon it so much the aspect of high and continuous elaboration.

His friend,--and sometimes associate in pastoral work,--Edward Irving, on the other hand, could not write a sermon if any one was in the room with him. Chalmers appears to have been specially endowed with that faculty of concentrated attention which is commonly regarded as one of the surest marks of the highest intellect, and which Alison so much admired in Wellington--as, for instance, on the day when he lay at San Christoval, in front of the French army, hourly expecting a battle, and wrote out, in the field, a long and minute memorial on the establishment of a bank at Lisbon on the principles of the English ones.

We read of Ercilla, whose epic poem, the Arancana, has admirers out of Spain, that he wrote it amidst the incessant toils and dangers of a campaign against barbarians, without shelter, and with nothing to write on but small scraps of waste paper, and often only leather; struggling at once against enemies and surrounding circumstances.

Louis de Cormantaigne, the distinguished French engineer, composed his treatise on fortification from notes written in the trenches and on the breaches, even under the fire of the enemy.

Delambr?was in Paris when it was taken by the allies in 1814, and is said to have worked at his problems with perfect tranquility from eight in the morning till midnight, in the continued hearing of the cannonade. "Such self-possession for study under that tremendous attack, and such absence of interest in the result of the great struggle, to say nothing of indifference to personal danger," is what one of his biographers confesses himself unable to understand. Small sympathy would the philosopher have had with the temperament of such a man, say, as Thomas Hood, who always wrote most at night, when all was quiet and the children were asleep. "I have a room to myself," exclaims Hood, triumphantly, in a letter describing a change of lodgings, "which will be worth ?0 a year to me,--for a little disconcerts my nerves." Mrs. Hood brought up the children, we learn from one of them, in a sort of Spartan style of education, on her husband's account, teaching them the virtues of silence and low voices.

Washington Irving was of a less morbid temperament, and his genial nature could put up with obstacles and obstructions neither few nor small; but even in his Diary we meet with such entries as this at Bordeaux, in 1825: "Harassed by noises in the house, till I had to go out in despair, and write in Mr. Guestier's library." It was upon the Essay on American Scenery that he was then engaged.

Unlike Maturin, who used to compose with a wafer pasted on his forehead, which was the signal that if any of his family entered the sanctum they must not speak to him, Scott allowed his children (like their mute playmates, Camp and the greyhounds) free access to his study, never considered their talk as any disturbance, let them come and go as pleased their fancy, was always ready to answer their questions, and when they, unconscious how he was engaged (writes the husband of one of them), entreated him to lay down his pen and tell them a story, he would take them on his knee, repeat a ballad or a legend, kiss them, and set them down again to their marbles or ninepins, and resume his labor as if refreshed by the interruption. There was nothing in that manly, sound, robust constitution akin to the morbid irritability of Philip in the poem:--

"When Philip wrote, he never seemed so well-- Was startled even if a cinder fell, And quickly worried."

Biographers of Mistress Aphra Behn make it noteworthy of that too facile penwoman that she could write away in company and maintain the while her share in the talk. Madame Roland managed to get through her memoirs with a semblance at least of unbroken serenity, though so often interrupted in the composition of them by the cries of victims in the adjoining cells, whom the executioners were dragging thence to the guillotine.

Madame de Sta, "even in her most inspired compositions," according to Madame Necker de Saussure, "had pleasure in being interrupted by those she loved." She was not, observed Lord Lytton, of the tribe of those who labor to be inspired; who darken the room and lock the door, and entreat you not to disturb them. Rather, she came of the same stock as George Sand's Olympe,

That Lord Castlereagh was able to write his despatches at the common table in the common room of a country house is not unjustly among the admiring reminiscences of a Septuagenarian (Countess Brownlow): "Once only we found the talking and laughter were too much for his power of abstraction, and then he went off into his own room, saying next morning at breakfast, 'You fairly beat me last night; I was writing what I may call the metaphysics of politics.'"

Celebrated in the "Noctes Ambrosian? is the Glasgow poet, Sandy Rogers, not less for his lyrics, one at least of which is pronounced by Christopher North to be "equal to anything of the kind in Burns," than for the fact that his verses--some of them, too, of a serious character--were thought out amidst the bustle and turmoil of factory labor, the din of the clanking steam-engine, and the deafening rattle of machinery, while the work of committing them to paper was generally performed amidst the squalling and clamor of children around the hearth, now in the noise of fractious contention, and anon exuberant with fun and frolic.

Tannahill, too, composed while plying the shuttle,--humming over the airs to which he meant to adapt new words; and, as the words occurred to him, jotting them down at a rude desk which he had attached to his loom, and which he could use without rising from his seat. But no more noteworthy example of the pursuit of authorship under difficulties--the difficulties of a narrow home--res augusta domi--is probably on record, in its simple, homely way, than that of Jean Paul, as During pictures him, sitting in a corner of the room in which the household work was being carried on--he at his plain writing-desk, with few or no books about him, but merely with a drawer or two containing excerpts and manuscripts; the jingle and clatter that arose from the simultaneous operations at stove and dresser no more seeming to disturb him than did the cooing of the pigeons which fluttered to and fro in the chamber, at their own sweet will.

Dr. Johnson delved at his dictionary in a poor lodging-house in London, with a cat purring near, and orange peel and tea at hand.

Moliere tested the comic power of his plays by reading them to an old servant.

Dr. William E. Channing used to perambulate the room while composing; his printers report that he made many revisions of the proof of his writings, so that before the words met the eyes of the public on the printed page the sentences were finished with the most elaborate minuteness.

Bloomfield, the poet, relates of himself that nearly one-half of his poem, "The Farmer's Boy," was composed without writing a word of it, while he was at work, with other shoemakers, in a garret.

Sharon Turner, author of the valuable "History of the Anglo-Saxons," who received a pension of $1,500 from the British government for his services to literature, wrote the third volume of "The Sacred History of the World" upon paper that did not cost him a farthing. The copy consisted of torn and angular fragments of letters and notes, of covers of periodicals and shreds of curling papers, unctuous with pomatum and bear's grease.

Mrs. Lizzie W. Champney writes absolutely without method. Her stories, she admits, have been penned in her nursery, with her baby in her lap, and a sturdy little boy standing on the rails of her chair and strangling her with his loving little arms. She works whenever and wherever she can find the opportunity; but the children are always put first.

George Ticknor, the Bostonian, found William Hazlitt living in the very house in which Milton dictated "Paradise Lost," and occupying the room where the poet kept the organ on which he loved to play. It was an enormous room, but furnished only with a table, three chairs, and an old picture. The most interesting thing that the visitor from Boston saw, except the occupant himself, was the white-washed walls. Hazlitt had used them as a commonplace book, writing on them in pencil scraps of brilliant thoughts, half-lines of poetry, and references. Hazlitt usually wrote with the breakfast things on the table, and there they remained until he went out, at four or five o'clock, to dinner. His pen was more to him than a mechanical instrument; it was also the intellectual wand by which he called up thoughts and opinions, and clothed them in appropriate language.

It was in a bookseller's back-shop, M. Nisard tells us, on a desk to which was fastened a great Newfoundland dog (who, by-the-bye, one day banged through the window of an upper room, desk and all, to join his master in the street below), that Armand Carrel, one moment absorbed in English memoirs and papers, another moment in caressing his four-footed friend, conceived and wrote his "History of the Counter Revolution in England." Mr. Walker, in this as in other respects "The Original," adopted a mode of composition which, says he, "I apprehend to be very different from what could be supposed, and from the usual mode. I write in a bedroom at a hotel, sitting upon a cane chair, in the same dress I go out in, and with no books to refer to but the New Testament, Shakespeare, and a pocket dictionary." Now and then, when much pressed for time, and without premeditation, and with his eye on the clock, he wrote some of his shorter essays at the Athenæm Club, at the same table where other members were writing notes and letters.

VI.

Aids to Inspiration.

Washington Irving's literary work was generally performed before noon. He said the happiest hours of his life were those passed in the composition of his different books. He wrote most of "The Stout Gentleman" while mounted on a stile, or seated on a stone, in his excursions with Leslie, the painter, 'round about Stratford-on-Avon,--the latter making sketches in the mean time. The artist says that his companion wrote with the greatest rapidity, often laughing to himself, and from time to time reading the manuscript aloud.

Dr. Darwin wrote most of his works on scraps of paper with a pencil as he travelled. But how did he travel? In a worn and battered "sulky," which had a skylight at the top, with an awning to be drawn over it at pleasure; the front of the carriage being occupied by a receptacle for writing-paper and pencils, a knife, fork, and spoon; while on one side was a pile of books reaching from the floor nearly to the front window of the carriage; on the other, by Mrs. Schimmel-penninck's account, a hamper containing fruit and sweetmeats, cream and sugar,--to which the big, burly, keen-eyed, stammering doctor paid attentions as devoted as he ever bestowed on the pile of books.

Alexander Kisfaludy, foremost Hungarian poet of his time, wrote most of his "Himfy" on horseback or in solitary walks; a poem, or collection of poems, that made an unprecedented sensation in Hungary, where, by the same token, Sandor Kisfaludy of that ilk became at once the Great Unknown.

Cujas, the object of Chateaubriand's special admiration, used to write lying flat on his breast, with his books spread about him.

Sir Henry Wotton is our authority for recording of Father Paul Sarpi that, when engaged in writing, his manner was to sit fenced with a castle of paper about his chair, and overhead; "for he was of our Lord of St. Albans' opinion, that 'all air is predatory' and especially hurtful when the spirits are most employed."

Rousseau tells us that he never could compose pen in hand, seated at a table, and duly supplied with paper and ink; it was in his promenades,--the promenades d'un solitaire,--amid rocks and woods, and at night, in bed, when he was lying awake, that he wrote in his brain; to use his own phrase, "J'閏 ris dans mon cerveau." Some of his periods he turned and re-turned half a dozen nights in bed before he deemed them fit to be put down on paper. On moving to the Hermitage of Montmorency, he adopted the same plan as in Paris,--devoting, as always, his mornings to the pen-work de la copie, and his afternoons to la promenade, blank paper, book, and pencil in hand; for, says he, "having never been able to write and think at my ease except in the open air, sule dio, I was not tempted to change my method, and I reckoned not a little on the forest of Montmorency becoming--for it was close to my door-- my cabinet de travail." In another place he affirms his sheer incapacity for meditation by day, except in the act of walking; the moment he stopped walking, he stopped thinking, too, for his head worked with, and owhatever intellectual problem is solved by Jean Jacques. His strength was not to sit still. His Reveries, by the way, were written on scraps of paper of all sorts and sizes, on covers of old letters, and on playing cards--all covered with a small, neat handwriting. He was as economical of material as was "Paper-sparing Pope" himself.

In some points Chateaubriand was intellectually, or, rather, sentimentally, related to Rousseau, but not in his way of using ink and paper.

Chateaubriand sat at a table well supplied with methodically arranged heaps of paper cut in sizes; and as soon as a page was blotted over in the biggest of his big handwriting,--according to M. de Marcullus, with almost as many drops of ink as words,--he tossed it aside, without using pounce or blotting-paper, to blot and be blotted by its accumulating fellows. Now and then he got up from this work, to look out of the window, or to pace the room, as if in quest of new ideas. The chapter finished, he collected all the scattered leaves, and revised them in due form--more frequently adding to than curtailing their fair proportions, and paying very special attention to the punctuation of his sentences.

Lessing's inherent nobility of intellect is said to have been typified in his manner of study. When in the act of composition he walked up and down till his eye was caught by the title of some book. He would open it, his brother tells us, and, if struck by some sentence which pleased him, he would copy it out; in so doing, a train of thought would be suggested, and this would be immediately followed up--provided his mood was just right.

The early morning would lure Jean Paul Richter to take out his ink-flask and write as he walked in the fragrant air. Such compositions as his "Dream of a Madman" he would set about by first seating himself at the harpsichord, and "fantasying" for a while on it, till the ideas, or "imaginings," came--which presently they would do with a rush.

Tradition, as we get it through the historian of the Clapham Sect, informs us that Wilberforce wrote his "Practical View" under the roof of two of his best friends, in so fragmentary and irregular a manner, that one of them, when at length the volume lay complete on the table, professed, on the strength of this experience, to have become a convert to the opinion that a fortuitous concourse of atoms might, by some felicitous chance, combine themselves into the most perfect of forms--a moss-rose or a bird of paradise.

Coleridge told Hazlitt that he liked to compose in walking over uneven ground, or breaking through the straggling branches of a copse-wood.

Sheridan composed at night, with a profusion of lights around him, and a bottle of wine by his side. He used to say: "If a thought is slow to come, a glass of good wine encourages it; and when it does come, a glass of good wine rewards it."

Lamartine, in the days of his prosperity, composed in a studio with tropical plants, birds, and every luxury around him to cheer the senses.

Berkeley composed his "Minute Philosopher" under the shade of a rock on

Newport Beach.

Burns wove a stanza as he ploughed the field.

Charlotte Bront?had to choose her favorable days for writing,--sometimes weeks, or even months, elapsing before she felt that she had anything to add to that portion of her story which was already written; then some morning she would wake up, and the progress of her tale lay clear and bright before her, says Mrs. Gaskell, in distinct vision; and she set to work to write out what was more present to her mind at such times than her actual life was. She wrote on little scraps of paper, in a minute hand, holding each against a piece of board, such as is used in binding books, for a desk,--a plan found to be necessary for one so short-sighted,--and this sometimes as she sat near the fire by twilight.

While writing "Jane Eyre" she became intensely concerned in the fortunes of her heroine, whose smallness and plainness corresponded with her own. When she had brought the little Jane to Thornfield, her enthusiasm had grown so great that she could not stop. She went on incessantly for weeks. At the end of this time she had made the minute woman conquer temptation, and in the dawn of the summer morning leave Thornfield. "After Jane left Thornfield, the rest of the book," says Miss Martineau, "was written with less vehemence and with more anxious care"--the world adds, "with less vigor and interest."

"Ouida" (Louise de la Ramses) writes in the early morning. She gets up at five o'clock, and, before she begins, works herself up into a sort of literary trance.

Professor Wilson, the Christopher North of Blackwood's Magazine, jotted down in a large ledger "skeletons," from which, when he desired an article, he would select one and clothe it with muscle and nerve. He was a very rapid writer and composer, but worked only when he liked and how he liked. He maintained that any man in good health might write an entire number of Blackwood's. He described himself as writing "by screeds"--the fit coming on about ten in the morning, which he encouraged by a caulker ("a mere nut-shell, which my dear friend the English opium-eater would toss off in laudanum"); and as soon as he felt that there was no danger of a relapse, that his demon would be with him the whole day, he ordered dinner at nine, shut himself up within triple doors, and set manfully to work. "No desk! An inclined plane--except in bed--is my abhorrence. All glorious articles must be written on a dead flat." His friend, the Ettrick Shepherd, used a slate.

Dr. Georg Ebers, professor at the University of Leipzig, Saxony, who is known all over the world as the author of novels treating of ancient Egyptian life, and as the writer of learned treatises on the country of the Khedives, prefers to work in the late evening hours until midnight when composing poetry, but favors daylight for labor on scientific topics. He makes a rough draft of his work, has this copied by an amanuensis, and then polishes and files it until it is satisfactory to him, that is, as perfect as he possibly can make it. He finds that tobacco stimulates him to work, and, therefore, he uses it when engaged in literary production. When he writes poetry, he is in the habit of sitting in an arm-chair, supporting a lap-board on his knee, which holds the paper; in this position he pens his lyrics. He imagines that he is more at liberty in this posture than when behind a writing desk. Ordinarily he writes with great ease, but sometimes the composition of a stirring chapter so mercilessly excites him that great beads of sweat appear upon his forehead, and he is compelled to lay down his pen, unable to write another line. He never writes unless he is in a suitable frame of mind, except it be on business matters. Sometimes, when laboring on topics of science, he works from ten to twelve hours at a stretch; he never spends more than three or four hours in succession on poetry.

Charles Reade's habit of working was unique. When he had decided on a new work he plotted out the scheme, situations, facts, and characters on three large sheets of pasteboard. Then he set to work, using very large foolscap to write on, working rapidly, but with frequent references to his storehouse of facts, in the scrap-books, which were ready at his hand. The genial novelist was a great reader of newspapers. Anything that struck him as interesting, or any fact which tended to support one of his humanitarian theories, was cut out, pasted in a large folio scrap-book, and carefully indexed. Facts of any sort were his hobby. From the scrap-books thus collected with great care he used to elaborate the "questions" treated of in his novels.

Like Charles Reade, Miss Anna Katherine Green is a believer in scrap-books, and culls from newspapers accounts of strange events. Out of such material she weaves her stories of crime and its detection.

Emile Zola, the graphic author of realistic fiction, carefully makes studies from life for his sensational works. He writes rapidly, smoking cigarettes the while. He is an inveterate smoker, and, if there is anything he likes better than tobacco, it is his beautiful country-house near Paris, where he receives daily a large circle of admiring friends.

Edward P. Roe, who, if we may rate success by the wide circulation of an author's books, was our most successful novelist, preferred the daytime for literary work, and rarely accomplished much in the evening beyond writing letters, reading, etc. When pressed with work he put in long hours at night. In the preface to "Without a Home," Rev. Mr. Roe presents some extremely interesting matter in regard to the causes which led to his authorship, and the methods of work by which he turned out so many well-constructed stories in so short a time. "Ten years ago," he says, "I had never written a line of a story, and had scarcely entertained the thought of constructing one. The burning of Chicago impressed me powerfully, and, obedient to an impulse, I spent several days among its smoking ruins. As a result, my first novel, 'Barriers Burned Away,' gradually took possession of my mind. I did not manufacture the story at all, for it grew as naturally as do the plants--weeds, some may suggest--on my farm. In the intervals of a busy and practical life, and also when I ought to have been sleeping, my imagination, unspurred and almost undirected, spun the warp and woof of the tale and wove them together.... I merely let the characters do as they pleased, and work out their own destiny. I had no preparation for the work beyond a careful study of the topography of Chicago and the incidents of the fire. For nearly a year my chief recreation was to dwell apart among the shadows created by my fancy, and I wrote when and where I could--on steamboats and railroad cars, as well as in my study.... When the book appeared I suppose I looked upon it much as a young father looks upon his first child. His interest in it is intense, but he knows well that its future is very doubtful." Mr. Roe always wrote from a feeling that he had something to say; and never "manufactured" a novel in his life. While writing he was absorbed in his work; and made elaborate studies for his novels. "I have visited," said he, in reference to "Without a Home," "scores of typical tenements. I have sat day after day on the bench with the police judges, and have visited the station-houses repeatedly. There are few large retail shops that I have not entered many times, and I have conversed with both employers and employees."

Mr. Roe did not make "outlines" or "skeletons" to any great extent, and when he did so, he did not follow them closely. Indeed, he often reversed his plan, satisfied that following an arbitrary outline makes both story and characters wooden. He held that the characters should control the author, not he them. He usually received the suggestion of a story unexpectedly, and let it take form in his mind and grow naturally, like a plant, for months, more often for years, before he began to write. He averred that after his characters were introduced he became merely the reporter of what they do, say, and think. He imagined that it was this spontaneity which, chiefly, made his books popular, and said that to reach intelligent people through fiction, the life portrayed must seem to them real and natural, and that this can scarcely be true of his characters if the author is forever imposing his arbitrary will upon them. Mr. Roe wrote in bound blank-books, using but one side of a sheet. This allowed ample space for changes and corrections, and the manuscript was kept in place and order. The novelist used tea, and especially coffee, to some extent as a stimulant, and smoked very mild cigars. But he rarely took coffee at his dinner, at six P.M., as it tended to insomnia. The author of "Barriers Burned Away" worked three or four hours before and two or three hours after lunch. On this point, however, he varied. When wrought up and interested in a scene, he usually completed it. In the after part of the day, when he began to feel weary, he stopped, and, if hard pressed, began work again in the evening. Once, many years ago, he wrote twenty-four hours at a stretch, with the aid of coffee. He did not force himself to work against inclination beyond a certain point. At the same time he fought against a tendency to "moods and tenses."

The German lyric poet, Martin Greif, writes only in the daytime, because he can conceive poetry only when walking in the woods, meadows, and lanes that form the environs of the Bavarian capital--Munich. During his excursions into the surrounding country, he notes down his thoughts, which he elaborates when he reaches his quiet study. He is not a ready versifier, and is compelled to alter a poem repeatedly before it receives his approbation. At work in the afternoon, he loves to smoke moderately; but he never uses stimulants. Generally work is hard to him, but sometimes--that is, rarely--he writes with unusual rapidity. As a professional writer, he must sometimes force himself to work and must mount the Pegasus in spite of disinclination, as when, for instance, a product of his pen has to be delivered on a certain date.

Emile Mario Vacano composed his writings at all times that gave him the impulse for doing so: at daybreak or in the night. With him it was the "whereabouts," not the hour, that made the essence. There was a mill belonging to a good friend of his, where he found his best inspirations amidst all the hubbub of horses, peasants, poultry, cows, pigeons, and country life. And he asserted that the name of his friend, Harry Salzer, of Stattersdorf, near St. Poelten, Lower Austria, ought to be joined to his. He said that his friend merited a great share of his "glories" by his hospitality as well as on account of his bright ideas. Vacano never made a plan in advance, but penned his novels, stories, essays, etc., as one writes a letter,--prima vista,-- never perusing again what he had written, be it good or bad. When writing he imbibed a good deal of beer, and was in the habit of using snuff. He did not regard writing as work. For him it was like a chat in pen and ink with friends. As for an inclination to work; as for a feeling that he had something to say, and must say it, come what will,--there was nothing of the sort in him. He said he hated romances, tales, and all the like, and wrote only to gain his "pain quotidien" and that he detested the humbug with all his heart and despised the mob that would read it. He declared that if he were a millionaire or simply wealthy, "he'd never take a pen in hand for bullying a stupid public with his nonsense."

Emile Richebourg writes his fascinating novels in a plain style, but, despite the absence of flowery language, is capable of expressing much feeling. The novel or drama is completed in his head before he writes a line. As the plot develops, the dialogues and events suggest themselves. When he has got to work he keeps right on, seldom re-reading what he has composed. He makes an outline of his book before beginning. He is in the habit of noting down on a piece of paper the names, ages, lodgings, etc., of the persons who are pictured in his novels, also the title of each chapter. Formerly he worked from eight to twelve hours a day, but never at night. Now he labors only five or six hours at the most, and always in the morning. Richebourg is an early riser, and goes to bed early in the evening. He gets up at six in the morning. At eight o'clock he drinks a bowl of warm milk without sugar, which constitutes his sole nourishment until dinner at noon. With him this is the principal meal of the day; and during its progress, according to his own confession, he finds a bottle of wine very agreeable. He eats but little in the evening. When at work he smokes continuously; always a pipe. He works with difficulty, yet with pleasure, and identifies himself, that is, when composing, with the personages whom he describes. During the afternoon he promenades in his garden, attends to his roses and other flowers, and trims the shrubs.

The study of Maurice Jokai, the great Hungarian romancer, is a perfect museum of valuable souvenirs and rare antiquities. Books, journals, and pamphlets cover tables, chairs, and walls; busts and statuettes, which stand about here and there, give the room the appearance of picturesque disorder. The portrait of his wife, in various sizes, adorns the space on the walls not taken up by the books. The top of his writing-table is full of bric-?brac, which leaves only sufficient room for the quarto paper upon which he pens his entertaining romances. He writes with little, fine pens, of so good a workmanship that he is enabled to write a four-volume novel with one pen. He always makes use of violet ink, to which he is so accustomed that he becomes perplexed when compelled, outside of his house, to resort to ink of another color. He claims that thoughts are not forthcoming when he writes with any other ink. When violet ink is not within reach, he prefers to write with a lead pencil, but he does so only when composing short stories and essays. For the composition of his romances, which generally fill from one to five volumes when printed, violet ink is indispensable. He rarely corrects his manuscripts, and they generally go to the printer as they were originally composed; they are written in a plain, legible hand; and are what one of the typographic fraternity would call "beautiful copy." One of the corners of his writing-desk holds a miniature library, consisting of neatly-bound note-books, which contain the outlines of his novels as they originated in his mind. When he has once begun a romance, he keeps right on till he puts down the final period; that is, he writes day by day till the novel is completed. Jokai says: "It often happens that I surround my hero with dangers, that enemies arise on all sides, and escape seems impossible. Then I often say to myself: 'I wonder how the fellow will get out of the scrape?'"

In his home, at Hartford, Conn., Mark Twain's workshop is in his billiard-room, at the top of the house, and when he grows tired of pushing the pen he rises and eases his muscles by doing some scientific strokes with the cue. He is a hard worker, and, like Trollope, believes that there is nothing like a piece of shoemaker's wax on the seat of one's chair to encourage good literary work. Ordinarily he has a fixed amount of writing for each day's duty. He rewrites many of his chapters, and some of them have been scratched out and interlined again and again.

Robert Waldmueller, a leading German novelist, who writes under the pseudonym of "Charles Eduard Duboc," works mostly from eight, nine, or ten o'clock in the morning until two o'clock in the afternoon, but never writes at night. Generally he does not plan his work beforehand. When at work he must be unmolested. In composition, he loves to change off, now producing poetry, now plays and essays, as his mood may direct. He writes with great ease and swiftness; and the many books which he has composed testify that he cannot justly be accused of indolence. He attributes his facility of expression to the discrimination which he has always exercised in the choice of books. In early boyhood he was already disgusted with Florian's sickly "Guillaume Tell," while Washington Irving's "Sketch-book" delighted him very much; he was also deeply impressed by the perusal of Homer's immortal epics. He adopted authorship when twenty-five years of age, and has followed it successfully ever since. Until then he was especially fond of composing music and of drawing and painting, but he lacked the time to perfect himself in these accomplishments. Yet, even to-day, he practices both arts occasionally as a pastime and for recreation.

The evening finds Dr. Johann Fastenrath, the poet, who writes as elegant Spanish as he does German, and who is as well-known in Madrid as he is in Cologne on the Rhine, at the writing-table. He never makes a skeleton beforehand of essays in his mother-tongue; but for compositions in French or Spanish he invariably makes an outline. One peculiarity which he has is to scribble his poems upon little scraps of paper. When writing prose in Spanish he divides the manuscript-paper in halves, so as to be able to make additions and to lengthen any particular sentence, for in the Spanish language artfully long periods are considered especially beautiful. He does not regard literary composition as work, and conceives poems faster than he can write them down. When he is at work absolute quiet must reign about him; he cannot bear noise of any kind. During the winter he works day for day at home, but in the summer he tolerates confinement no longer, and whenever he composes at this time it is always in the open air. From autumn till spring he writes from six to seven hours a day.

Adolf Streckfusz, a German novelist, prefers to write in the afternoon and evening, and attains the greatest speed in composition at night. He makes no plan beforehand, but revises his manuscript at least twice after completion. He often allows the cigar which he smokes when at work to go out, but lights it mechanically from time to time, so that the floor of his study is sometimes covered with dozens of thrown-away lucifers after working hours. When writing, his cigar is as indispensable to him as his pen. He can do without neither. Formerly he could work with extraordinary facility, but now, with increasing age, a few hours' work at times tires him out so much that he must, of necessity, take a rest. As with many other authors, a sense of duty often impels him to work; but almost always, after a beginning is made, he composes with pleasure. The time which he devotes daily to literary work varies. He never works more than eight hours, but rarely less than three or four hours a day.

The author of "The Lady or the Tiger" and many other short stories--Frank R. Stockton--always works in the morning, and not at any other time. In writing a short story, such as is published in a single number of a magazine, he usually composes the whole story, description, incident, and even the dialogue, before writing a word of it. In this way the story is finished in his mind before it is begun on paper. While engaged in other writing he has carried in his memory for several months as many as three stories, each ready to be put upon paper as soon as he should have an opportunity. When he is writing a longer story, he makes in his mind a general outline of the plot, etc.; and then he composes three or four chapters before he begins to write; when these are finished, he stops writing until some more are thought out: he never composes at the point of the pen. He does not write any of his manuscripts himself; they are all written from his dictation. Stockton is very fond of working in the summer in the open air, and a great many of his stories have been dictated while lying in a hammock. He usually works from about ten in the morning until one P. M., but he spends no time at the writing-desk, except when he writes letters, which he never does in his working hours. Some years ago he used to work very differently, being occupied all day with editorial work, and in the evening with literary work; but his health would not stand this, and he, therefore, adopted his present methods. He works regularly every day, whether he feels like it or not; but when he has set his mind on a subject, it is generally not long before he does feel like it.

Dr. Leopold Chevalier de Sacher-Masoch generally used to work at night in former years, but now writes by daylight only, preferably in the morning. He is the author of a great many graphic stories about Galicia, and lives at Leipsic, surrounded by a coterie of admiring friends. He makes an accurate outline; then pens his novel word for word till it is finished, whereupon it is handed to the printer as it is, not a word being altered, added, or erased. He is not in the habit of using stimulating drinks or tobacco when at work, and leads altogether a temperate life. He has an innate predilection for fur, and declares that fur worn by a beautiful woman exercises a magic spell over him. Formerly he had a pretty black cat that used to lie on his knees or sleep on his writing-desk when he was at work. Now, when he writes, a red velvet lady's-jacket, with a fur lining of sable and borders of the same material, lies near at hand upon a divan. Although he is ordinarily good-natured, his anger is easily provoked by any disturbance during working hours. Composition is mere play to him after he has begun, but the first lines of a new work always are penned with difficulty. When he writes without an inclination, he is, as a rule, dissatisfied with the result. Generally he spends from three to four hours at the writing-desk and devotes the rest of the day to recreation.

Dr. Julius Stinde, who is responsible for that excellent German satire, "Die Familie Buchholz," never works by lamplight, if he can possibly avoid it. He writes on large sheets, of quarto size, and never makes an outline; the compositor gets the manuscript as it was written, with a few, but not many, alterations. Whatever is not satisfactory to the author is thrown into the waste-paper basket, which, in consequence, is pretty large. While at work he takes a pinch of snuff from time to time, which, he asserts, has a beneficial action on the eyes that are taxed by incessant study and composition. When he treats of scientific topics, a few glasses of Rhine wine tend to induce the proper mood; he finds the "Johannisgarten," a wine grown at Musbach in the palatinate of the Rhine, especially valuable for this purpose. He composes humorous work most easily after a very simple breakfast, consisting of tea and bread. He is in the habit of often changing the kinds of paper, pens, pen-holders, ink, and even ink-stands, which he uses; and loves to see fresh flowers on his writing-desk. He writes with greater facility in fine, sunny weather than on dark, gloomy days. That is the reason why he prefers, on cloudy days, to write in the evening. He declares that he would rather stop writing for days and weeks than to compose without inclination, and he tells us that whenever he attempts to work "sans inclination" as the French say, the result is unsatisfactory, and the effort strains both mind and body. He seldom spends more than eight hours a day at the writing-table.

To the many with whom it is customary to do literary work in the daytime must be added Johannes Nordmann, one of Vienna's most able novelists and newspaper men. He writes more during the winter than in the summer time, most of which he spends in travelling. He never recopies prose. For poems, however, he first makes an outline, and then files the verse till it receives his approbation. While driving the "quill," he smokes cigars. He writes with remarkable speed and ease after the subject in hand has ripened in his thoughts. He often forces himself to do newspaper work, when he would fain do anything else; and is totally unable to compose fiction or poetry when not disposed to.

Moncure D. Conway burns daylight, never the midnight oil, and rarely the evening oil. Generally he works with his pen eight hours a day, tries to take two walks, and in the evening to get some amusement,--billiards or the theatre, of which he is very fond. He smokes as he begins work, but does not keep it up, and uses no other stimulant at work. He loves work, and never has had to force himself to labor. He generally makes some outline of what he means to write, but often leaves it, finding his thoughts developed by stating them. Conway has to be alone when writing, but does not care for noise outside of his study. He is a slow writer, and is always waiting on a nursery of slowly-maturing subjects.

Kate Field, the well-known editor and lecturer, prefers the daytime for literary work, for the reason, she says, that the brain is far clearer in the morning than at any other time. This refers, of course, to a normal brain, independent of stimulants. She thinks that, under pressure, night work in journalism is often more brilliant than any other; but that it is exceptional. She makes no outline in advance; and never uses stimulants, hot water excepted. She has no particular habit when at work, except the habit of sticking to it; and has no specified hours for work. She spends no time at a desk, as she writes in her lap, a habit which was also a peculiarity of Mrs. Browning. Miss Field maintains that it is far easier for her, and prevents round shoulders, and is also better for the lungs. She has forced herself to write at times, and does not believe in waiting for ideas "to turn up."

E. Vely, one of the best of the female novelists of Germany, however, believes in inspirations, and does not take a pen in hand unless disposed to write. Four hours in the forenoon are spent in composition, while the afternoon and evening are given up to pastime, exercise, and study. While at work she hates to be interrupted, and insists upon absolute stillness about her. She always sends her original manuscript to the printer.

And now we come to one who recently joined the great majority, one who, although he has gone the way of all mortals, still lives, whose name is not only found on the long list of the illustrious dead, but is also graven in golden letters on the record of the age: Dr. Alfred Meissner. It was his wont to do the imaginative part of his work in the stillness of the night, either in an easy chair--smoking a cigar--or in bed, in which he used to pass several hours sleepless almost every day. He used to sit down to write in the morning and quit at noon. Early in his literary career this distinguished Austrian novelist discovered that composition in the night-time, that is, the mechanical part of it, would not agree with him, that it was too great a strain on his nervous system, and so wisely concluded to write only by daylight. He was unable to comprehend how anybody could write a novel--a very intricate work--without making alterations and erasures subsequently in the original manuscripts. It appeared to him as if an artist would not make a sketch of his projected picture first, but would begin immediately to paint in oil and make no changes afterward. He cited the example of Raphael and Titian, who, although they were talented artists, made numerous sketches before they began a painting. Dr. Meissner first made a detailed outline of his work, which he elaborated with great care. While copying this second manuscript he was enabled to make a great many alterations, and to strike out everything that was unsuitable. Practically every production of his pen was written three times.

Sometimes Meissner would work with great ease, sometimes with difficulty. The composition of chapters that were full of stirring incidents, violent passions, or perilous situations used to excite him intensely, and progressed by degrees; whereas other chapters were written with great facility and swiftness. He wrote only when he was compelled to by his creative faculty, that urged him to set down what he had to say. He was a very diligent author, and left many books to keep his memory green and constantly endear him to the hearts of the people.

Dr. A. Glaser, the German novelist, dictates all his stories to a private secretary, a luxury which few Teutonic authors can afford. Ordinarily he writes in the daytime, but when deeply interested in some new work he keeps right on till late at night. Music, especially classic music, exerts a great influence on the products of his pen. When his work progresses slowly, a complication is not easily solved, or a character becomes somewhat indistinct, music, that is, oratorios and symphonies, invariably sets all matters right and dispels all difficulties. He never writes with greater facility or rapidity than when he has heard the music of Handel, Bach, or Beethoven just before sitting down to write.

What little literary work John Burroughs does is entirely contingent upon his health. If he is not feeling absolutely well, with a good appetite for his food, a good appetite for sleep, for the open air, for life generally, there is no literary work for him. If his sleep has been broken or insufficient, the day that follows is lost to his pen. He leads a sane and simple life: goes to bed at nine o'clock and gets up at five in summer and at six in winter; spends half of each day in the open air; avoids tea and coffee, tobacco, and all stimulating drinks; adheres mainly to a fruit and vegetable diet, and always aims to have something to do which he can do with zest. He is fond of the mild excitement of a congenial talk, of a conversation with friends, of a walk in the fields or woods, of a row on the river, of the reading of a good book. During working-hours he likes to regale himself with good buttermilk, in which, he avers, there is great virtue. He writes for the most part only in fall and winter; writing best when his chimney draws best. He composes only when writing is play. His working hours, when he does write, are from nine or ten A. M. to two or three P. M. Then he wants his dinner, and after that a brisk walk of four or five miles, rain or shine. In the evening he reads or talks with his friends.

When Charles Deslys, the French novelist, begins to write he has a very indistinct idea of what he is about to compose; but after a while, becoming interested in the work, he writes with increasing pleasure, and the clouds which shut out the subject from view quickly clear away. He never makes an outline beforehand. He does not use stimulating drinks, but smokes much; and seldom works more than four or five hours at a time. At Nice, where he spends his winters now, he writes all the morning, from eight o'clock until noon, at the window, which is opened wide to let in the sunlight. In summer he always works in the open air, preferably at the seashore or in the woods. In this way he composed his first romances, novels, and songs, writing them down first in a note-book, which he always carried with him. Sometimes he dictated to a secretary. He has lost that faculty, and now must write down everything himself, either at his table or his writing-desk.

John Fiske, the evolutionist, describes himself as follows:--

"I am forty-three years old; six feet in height, girth of chest, forty-six inches; waist, forty-four inches; head, twenty-four inches; neck, eighteen inches; arm, sixteen inches; weight, 240 pounds; complexion, florid; hair, auburn; beard, red."

Professor Fiske is a fine specimen of manhood: he is alert and active, possesses a voracious appetite, a perfect digestion, and ability to sleep soundly. He works by day or night indifferently. His method, like General Grant's, is to "keep hammering." Sometimes he makes an outline first; but scarcely ever changes a word once written. He very seldom tastes coffee or wine, or smokes a cigar; but he drinks beer freely, and smokes tobacco in a meerschaum pipe nearly all the time when at work. He has been in the habit of working from twelve to fifteen hours daily since he was twelve years old. John Fiske is one of the healthiest of men, and never has a headache or physical discomfort of any sort. He prefers to work in a cold room, 55?to 60?F., and always sits in a draft when he can find one. He wears the thinnest clothes he can find, both in winter and summer. Despite this absence of precautions, he catches cold only once in three or four years, and then not severely. He never experienced the feeling of disinclination for work, and, therefore, has never had to force himself. If he feels at all dull when at work, he restores himself by a half-hour at the piano.

Ernest Wichert, who, besides being an honored member of the bar of Germany, is a celebrated novelist, courts the muses from eight o'clock in the morning until two in the afternoon. After five P. M. he attends to his correspondence and daily professional duties. Only two forenoons in the week are taken up by his duties as judge of the superior court at Koenigsberg, Prussia. He never copies a romance or novel once written, but leaves a margin for alterations and additions. When a sentence--not a judicial one--

presents any difficulty, he writes it out hastily on a small piece of paper before he puts it down in the manuscript. He is in the habit of revising and copying dramatic work at least three times before he submits it to a stage-manager. He is very much addicted to the use of tobacco, and smokes a pipe and a cigar alternately. He smokes at all times of the day, even during working-hours. Generally he sits down to write; but cannot bear to have a pen in hand when thinking about the subject of his work. He is accustomed to walk up and down the room until his thoughts have assumed a definite form. He works sometimes from five to six hours successively. He cannot write when anybody is in the room, and, therefore, always locks the doors before he sits down to his work. Literary labor is such a necessity to Wichert that he invariably feels uncomfortable when he has finished one work without beginning another immediately.

Many of the friends of Jules Claretie, the famous novelist, often are at a loss to account for his great fertility, and cannot see how he manages to do all that he succeeds in doing. When this question was once asked of the author, he replied, smilingly: "I am used to working, love to work, and work regularly--without excess, and with constant pleasure. Work is, with certain natures, one of the forms of health." Claretie's pen is put in motion only in the daytime; at night it rests, like the genial man himself. When the author feels indisposed, he does not write except for journals to which matter must be supplied on a certain date; attacks of neuralgia and nervous headache often interfere with his work. When at work he is in the habit of humming various tunes without being conscious of it. When work is easy to him, he sings; but when it is difficult, a dead silence reigns in his study. Sometimes work proves exceedingly hard to be done in the beginning, but the longer he writes the easier it becomes. Claretie notes down all ideas that come to his mind, utilizing them afterward for his novels. He also makes a detailed outline of his romances; but his journalistic articles are composed at the point of the pen. He is a very fast writer, and the ink on one page is often not quite dry before another is begun.

Hermann Rollet, a distinguished Austrian author, writes on scientific topics in the evening as well as in the day-time. With him poetry is evolved, almost without exception, in the dead of night, when he lies awake after having slept a few hours. He invariably makes an outline, and when his manuscript is finished he improves it as much as possible. There must be no noise in the room where he works; outside din, however, does not affect him. When Rollet has a clear conception of the subject in hand, work is mere play to him; otherwise, it is difficult indeed. The author has one great peculiarity, which is seldom met with, and has, I think, never been noted before. When composing poetry, it appears to him as if he only removes by the act of writing the covering from something that has been concealed, and he looks upon the resulting poem as if he had not produced it, as if it had been in existence before, and as if he had but revealed it. Thus generally his best songs are produced. Sometimes he dreams of a poem, verse for verse, line for line. If he happens to wake up at the time, and strikes a light, he is able to write down literally the poem of which he dreamt. Frequently he forgets all about his dream after it is written down, and is then greatly astonished in the morning to find a finished poem on his writing-table. He says that he could more easily split wood or break stones than to write without inclination. He has to force himself merely to copy what he has written.

VI.

Favorite Habits of Work.

John G. Whittier, our noble Quaker poet, used to say that he never had any method. "When I felt like it," he said once, "I wrote, and I neither had the health nor the patience to work afterward over what I had written. It usually went as it was originally completed."

Whittier preferred the daytime--and the morning, in fact--for writing, and used no stimulants whatever for literary labor. He made no outline or skeleton of his work--and claimed that his verses were made as the Irishman made his chimney--by holding up one brick and putting another under. He was subject to nervous headache all his life, and for this reason often had to force himself to work when he would rather have rested, especially while he was associate editor of the National Era and other papers.

Philipp Galen, the German novelist, composes during the daytime, and sometimes labors till ten o'clock in the evening. He makes an outline of his story before he prepares the "copy" for the press. He requires no stimulants at work, but when he is through he relishes a glass of wine. He has a habit of perambulating the room when engaged in meditation about a new book, and he writes with remarkable rapidity. He never puts pen to paper without inclination, because, as he says, he always feels disposed to do literary work. Formerly he worked daily from twelve to fourteen hours; now he spends only from six to eight hours at the writing-desk every day.

W. D. Howells always keeps his manuscript six or seven months ahead of the time for publication. Being of a nervous disposition, he could not rely on himself to furnish matter at short notice. When it is possible, he completes a book before giving a page of it to a magazine. He finds the morning to be the best time for brain-labor. He asserts that the first half of the day is the best part of a man's life, and always selects it for his working hours. He usually begins at nine and stops at one, and manages in that time to write about a dozen manuscript pages. After that he enjoys his leisure; that is, he reads, corrects proof, walks about, and pays visits. When he went to Venice as the United States consul he soon threw off the late-hour habits to which he was accustomed as a journalist. There was so little to keep him employed, and the neighborhood was so quiet and delightful, that he began doing his work in the morning, and he has continued the habit ever since. He does not generally make a "skeleton" of his work; in fact, he almost never does. He says that he leans toward indolence, and always forces himself more or less to work, keeping from it as long as he can invent any excuse. He often works when he is dull or heavy from a bad night, and finds that the indisposition wears off. Howells rarely misses a day from any cause, and, for a lazy man, as he calls himself, is extremely industrious.

Georgiana M. Craik never, except on the rarest occasions, wrote at night. She did not always make an outline of her books beforehand, but generally did so. She wrote from nine A. M. until two P. M. in winter, and in summer she seldom wrote at all. When she once began to write a book, she worked at it steadily four or five hours every day, without any regard to inclination.

Dr. Alfred Friedmann, a witty Austrian journalist, writes his brilliant articles at one sitting. He makes few corrections, and, sometimes, before the ink is dry on the "copy," off it goes to the printer. Whenever he feels in need of refreshment, he gets up from his writing-desk and has recourse to a wine-bottle near by. He never performs literary labor unless he is inclined to work. Sometimes he does not write for weeks, and then again he writes half a book at a time.

J. Scherr, the noted professor of the University of Zurich, Switzerland, who is a novelist as well as an historian, spends his forenoon at his writing-desk. He works standing, and writes, when in good health, with wonderful facility. Formerly, he often used to work as long as ten hours, but now he devotes only three or four hours a day to literary work.

Thomas Wentworth Higginson composes always in the daytime, never at night. He sometimes makes an outline. He uses no stimulants while at work, or at any time. He writes for from three to five hours a day. He sometimes forces himself to "drive the quill," but rarely, generally enjoying literary work very much.

Ludwig Auzengruber, the Austrian storyteller, never writes at night. He always makes an outline of his work at the beginning, and is addicted to tobacco, which he consumes when at work. He is in the habit of walking up and down the room when elaborating a new story, and never writes down a sentence before he has pronounced it aloud. Auzengruber is a very industrious man, and sometimes writes for as many as eleven hours a day.

Gerhard von Amyntor, who is one of the best known of German authors, is also a very diligent writer. He composes for from three to four hours every morning, but rarely in the evening, and never at night. The afternoon and evening are spent in reading or conversation, or in revising that which he has written in the forenoon. He never makes a skeleton of his work, but his manuscripts are copied before they reach the printer. Tobacco is indispensable to him when he is producing poetry. He works standing, and in solitude. The production, in the mind, of novels and fiction generally is easy to him, but the mechanical labor of writing down the product of his imagination he deems sad drudgery, because he is affected by writers' cramp, and he never sets pen to paper unless he feels disposed to.

Walt Whitman closely adhered to his home and rooms. His income was just sufficient to make both ends meet, but he used to say it was adequate to the wants of a poet. He declared that wealth and luxury would destroy his working force. The poet once wrote: "Twelve years ago I came to Camden to die; but every day I went into the country, and, naked, bathed in sunshine, lived with the birds and the squirrels, and played in the water with the fishes.

I recovered my health from Nature. Strange how she carries us through periods of infirmity, into the realms of freedom and health."

In contradistinction to the majority of authors, Hermann Herberg, German novelist and journalist, drives the pen at night. He invariably makes an outline of his work to start with, and when he is engaged in writing, he sips coffee and smokes. To him literary work is a holiday task; yet he never writes unless he is in the proper frame of mind, spending on the average three hours a day at the writing table.

The method of Louisa May Alcott was a very simple one. She never had a study; and an old atlas on her knee was all the desk she cared for. Any pen, any paper, any ink, and any quiet place contented her. Years ago, when necessity drove her hard, she used to sit for fourteen hours at her work, doing about thirty pages a day, and scarcely tasting food until her daily task was done. She never copied. When the idea was in her head, it flowed into words faster than she could write them down, and she seldom altered a line. She had the wonderful power of carrying a dozen plots for months in her mind, thinking them over whenever she was in the mood, to be developed at the proper time. Sometimes she carried a plan thus for years. Often, in the dead of night, she lay awake and planned whole chapters, word for word, and when daylight came she had only to write them down. She never composed in the evening. She maintained that work in the early hours gives morning freshness to both brain and pen, and that rest at night is a necessity for all who do brain work. She never used stimulants of any kind. She ate sparingly when writing, and only the simplest food, holding that one cannot preach temperance if one does not practice it. Miss Alcott affirmed that the quality of an author's work depends much on his habits, and that sane, wholesome, happy, and wise books must come from clean lives, well-balanced minds, spiritual insight, and a desire to do good.

Very few of the stories of the author of "Little Women" were written in Concord, her home. This peaceful, pleasant place, the fields of which are classic ground, utterly lacked inspiration for Miss Alcott. She called it "this dull town," and when she had a story to write she went to Boston, where she shut herself up in a room, and emerged only when she could show a completed work.

August Niemann, the German novelist, devotes the forenoon to literary work, but never burns midnight-oil on his writing-desk. He prepares his manuscript at the outset for the press, never making a plan beforehand. He writes with great facility, but only when he feels like it; when disinclined, he does not touch a pen--sometimes he will not write for weeks. When he is especially interested in a topic, he is apt to write for from four to six hours at a stretch; ordinarily he spends two, or, at the most, three, hours a day at the writing-table.

Victor Blenhgen, one of the most noted German authors, prefers the daytime, especially the early morning, for literary labor; and whenever he is compelled to work at night, in order to meet engagements, he does so after ten o'clock. He never makes a skeleton of his work, but when the manuscript is completed, he files away at it, and even makes alterations in the proof-sheets. While at work he smokes incessantly, and is so accustomed to the stimulating effects of tobacco that he cannot get along without it. He walks up and down the room while meditating on the plots of his stories. When he elaborates them everything must be quiet about him, for every loud noise, especially music, agitates him, and renders work impossible. Blanhgen is a ready writer, and conception and composition are both easy to him. He always forces himself to write. When he is beginning, he struggles hard to overcome his repugnance, until he is interested in the work, when he composes with increasing pleasure and rapidity. On the average, he writes for from three to six hours daily, but never more than three hours at a time. When he sits down to the desk he has but a faint idea of the novel which he is about to write, being incapable of working out the details of a story in his mind, as some authors are able to do; but with the ink the thoughts begin to flow, and all difficulties are surmounted.

Lucy Larcom declared that she never thought of herself as an author, and during most of her life her occupation was that of a teacher. She wrote always before she taught, and in the intervals of leisure she had,--she used to say because her head and pen would not keep still. She always wished for more leisure to write, but was obliged to do something that insured an immediate return in money,--in fact, she had always to "work for a living." So, it was her habit to take a book or a portfolio in her lap, and write when and where she could. She did not write at night, because, she said, she had learned that she must sleep. She often forced herself to write, sometimes through an entire day, although the result was not usually so satisfactory to herself. She used to keep writing, even if she felt a little ill and tired, because of the imperative "must," and because she could forget her bad feelings in her subject. She began to write as a little child,--verses chiefly,--and always preferred writing to doing anything else. Most of the things she wrote seemed to her to come of themselves, poems especially.

To the large number of those who prefer the daytime to the artificial light of the evening or the night must be added Rudolf von Gottschall, German historian, novelist, and essayist. While at work he is in the habit--that is at times--of chewing paper. He writes with ease and great speed. He often composes when disinclined to work, compelled by his occupation as a critic and journalist. Only when he is writing poetry he must be in good spirits. He devotes about five hours a day to literary work, exclusive of letter-writing and the discharge of his editorial duties.

Before committing her manuscripts to the press, the novelist, Marian Tenger (a pseudonym which stands for the name of a lady of the highest German aristocracy), reads them over repeatedly, and makes many alterations. It seems incredible to her that any author, who is attached to his profession, should write fair copy at once, making no skeleton of his work whatever. She invents dialogues most easily when she is perambulating the room. When disinclined to write, she refrains from touching a pen. Sometimes weeks elapse before she resumes her usual occupation--writing; but when she does so, it is with delight. She never writes for more than five hours daily.

Oliver Wendell Holmes prefers the morning from nine o'clock until noon for work. He used to write evenings, but of late he has not done so. He sometimes plans his work beforehand, but is apt to deviate more or less from the outline he has laid down. He uses no stimulants at his work, unless his cup of coffee is so considered. He spends sometimes two or three, sometimes four or five, hours a day at his writing-table. He very often forces himself to write when he has an uncompleted task before him. He must have a pen in his hand when he is composing in prose or verse--it seems a kind of conductor, without which his thoughts will not flow continuously in proper order.

Julius Wolffe, the German poet, belongs to those who never work at night.

He writes from early in the morning until the late hours of the afternoon. He makes an outline, which, however, is almost equivalent to fair copy, since very few additions and alterations are ever made. While at work he moderately smokes cigars. When he is absorbed in cogitation on a subject in hand, he often walks up and down his room. He writes with great facility, for he never treats of topics that are not congenial to him. He is a very industrious man; every day finds him at his writing-desk, where he spends from eight to nine hours out of the twenty-four.

The work of Edmund Gosse being multiform and very pressing, he has no choice between the daytime and the night, and must use both. The central hours of the day being given up to his official business for the government, which consists of translation from the various European languages, only the morning and the evening remain for literary work. His books have mainly been written between eight and eleven P. M., and corrected for the press between nine and ten A. M. He finds the afternoon almost a useless time. In his estimation, the physical clockwork of the twenty-four hours seems to run down about four P. M.,--at least, such is his experience. He makes no written skeleton or first draft. His first draft is what goes to the printers, and commonly with very few alterations. He rounds off his sentences in his head before committing them to paper. He uses no stimulant at work. He drinks wine twice a day, but after dinner he neither eats nor drinks. He has found this habit essential to his health and power of work. The only exception he makes is that, as he is closing for the night,--a little before eleven o'clock,--he takes several cups of very strong tea, which he has proved by experience to be by far the best sedative for his nerves. If he goes to bed immediately after this strong tea, at the close of a hard day's work, he generally sleeps soundly almost as soon as his head is on the pillow. Coffee keeps him awake, and so does alcohol. He has tried doing without wine, but has always returned to it with benefit. He has entirely given up tobacco, which never suited him. He can work anywhere, if he is not distracted. He has no difficulty in writing in unfamiliar places--the waiting-room of a railway station or a rock on the seashore suits him as well (except for the absence of books of reference) as the desk in his study. He cannot do literary or any other brain-work for more than three hours on a stretch, and believes that a man who will work three hours of every working-day will ultimately appear to have achieved a stupendous result in bulk, if this is an advantage. But, then, he must be rapid while he is at work, and must not fritter away his resources on starts in vain directions. Gosse is utterly unable to write to order,--that is to say, on every occasion. He can generally write, but there are occasions when for weeks together he is conscious of an invincible disinclination, and this he never opposes. Consequently, he is by temperament unfitted for journalism, in which he has, he thinks, happily, never been obliged to take any part. As for Mr. Gosse's verse, it gets itself written at odd times, wholly without rule or precedent, and, of course, cannot be submitted to rule; But his experience is that the habit of regular application is beneficial to the production of prose.

Felix Dahn, whose fertile fancy conjures up romances of life in ancient Rome, always writes by the light of day. He writes with great facility and rapidity; and devotes nine hours a day to literary work. His manuscript goes to the printer as it is originally composed, and he seldom alters a line after it is once committed to paper.

Albert Traeger, a celebrated German poet, writes in the afternoon,--after three o'clock, by preference. When composing prose, he writes fair copy at once; for poems, however, he makes an outline, which is hardly ever altered, since he completes every line in his head before he writes it down. While at work he constantly smokes very strong cigars, and is in the habit of sipping black coffee from time to time. The poet is a ready writer, but never pens a single sentence unless he feels disposed to work. Sometimes months pass before he takes up the neglected pen again.

That excellent writer of short stories, Sarah Orne Jewett, composes in the afternoon. She does not make a formal outline of her work, but has a rough plan of it in her own head, depending most upon a knowledge of the chief characters. She writes for about four hours a day, and often finds the first ten or fifteen minutes' work an effort, but after that she can almost always go on easily.

Thomas Hardy prefers the night for working, but finds the use of daytime advisable, as a rule. He follows no plan as to outline, and uses no stimulant excepting tea. His habit is to remove boots or slippers as a preliminary to work. He has no definite hours for writing, and only occasionally works against his will.

W. H. Riehl, who, besides being a professor at the University of Munich, is a famous novelist, always writes by daylight. He carefully outlines his work beforehand, and repeatedly revises it before it is printed. When engaged in the labor of composition, he smokes one cigar--no more. He invents easily, but is very painstaking when writing down his thoughts, mercilessly erasing whatever does not suit him. He takes a pen to hand whenever he has a leisure moment, sometimes in the morning, sometimes in the afternoon, as circumstances permit.

The renowned divine, Karl Gersk, who is the author of by far the best German religious poems, as a rule makes an outline before composing poetry, but writes down prose at once. When his attention is taken up by an interesting topic, he is in the habit of curling, absent-mindedly, one of his occipital locks about the left index finger. He rarely writes for more than six hours a day, and then only when he feels especially disposed to work.

The author of "St. Olave" always writes in the daytime; namely, from nine A. M. to one P. M.; and does not make any outline first, but only two copies, which are improved afterward, the first copy being written in pencil, and the second in ink. The second manuscript is revised and corrected. Day by day, this knight of the pen writes during the stated time, unless prevented by illness or unexpected engagements, and does not wait for "feeling disposed," but goes steadily on.

R. E. Francillon prefers working at night, when both ideas and words come most fluently. He always works at night, and sometimes all night, when he works against time. He has not then to conquer an unwillingness to work which besets him at other hours. Next to the night-time, he prefers the afternoon, to which circumstances practically confine him. This refers to imaginative work. With regard to journalistic and critical work and study, it is just the reverse, and he prefers the morning. He never makes a skeleton of his work. He has tried the skeleton method, but found it useless, and broke away from it soon after starting. He finds that incident suggests incident, and characters develop themselves. Of course, he starts with a motive (in the technical sense), and a general drift and color, and the salient points of leading characters. He uses no stimulant when at work, except tobacco in the form of cigarettes, which he smokes all the time, whatever he is doing, even when writing a letter. Pen and cigarette are inseparable; but he smokes very little when not working, and next to nothing when taking a holiday. His hours of work depend very much on necessity. He is engaged on a newspaper from nine A. M. till one P. M. The afternoon and evening are devoted to fiction or whatever other work he has on hand. Practically he is at his desk all day, an industry which is rendered possible by frequent change of work. He constantly forces himself to work, dead against inclination; and, though it may seem strange, it constantly happens that the less the original inclination, the better the result, and vice versa. Francillon has no faith whatever in writing upon inclination, and maintains that even if little comes of working when disinclined, the little is something and prevents the want of inclination lasting, besides preventing one from yielding easily. He is perfectly indifferent to outside noise, and, indeed, to almost everything that most people find a trial to the nerves--except conversation in the same room. He has worked with music playing in the same room, and has not even noticed it.

Hubert H. Bancroft, the historian of the Pacific coast, works day and evening, with little interruption, except as he takes a walk or rides for exercise occasionally in the afternoon. He determines that a certain amount of work shall be accomplished within so many hours, days, and weeks, and so is always stimulated and successfully accomplishes the allotted task. He frequently writes when not disposed to work.

Richard Schmidt Cabanis, the German humorist, has often spent whole nights at the writing-desk. When composing poetry he makes an outline beforehand, otherwise not. Before his manuscript goes to press he carefully revises it and strikes out a great deal. He is very fond of French red wine, which he imbibes occasionally when writing, but which he must often forego in obedience to the advice of his physicians. The only peculiarity of which he is possessed is that he cannot compose unless he is alone, and he scorns even dumb company during working hours.

Margaret Eytinge very much prefers the morning for writing, and generally spends from eight o'clock until eleven or twelve at her desk. Of course, she often works in the afternoon, and sometimes, though very rarely, at night. But at those times she only revises and copies. She makes a slight sketch of her poem or story first--a sketch written so hastily that it would be impossible for anybody but herself to decipher it, and she has found trouble in making it out herself at times. Then she proceeds to clothe this skeleton, an operation which is never completed satisfactorily until after at least three times trying.

She always makes it a point to produce clean manuscripts. She cannot write at all with people about her, or in an unfamiliar place, and must be in her own room, at her own desk, and secure from interruption.

That astute author of innumerable novels, Charlotte M. Yonge, never works at night. She does not write any outline of her tales. She has such an outline in her mind, but is guided by the way the characters shape themselves. She generally composes from about 10.30 A. M. to 1.30 P. M., taking odd times later in the day for proofs and letters. Having good health, she is seldom indisposed for work; if she is, she takes something mechanical, such as translating or copying.

Dr. Karl Frenzel, editor of one of the leading Berlin newspapers, has to struggle hard at first to overcome his unwillingness to compose, but after he has written for some time any aversion which he may have experienced disappears. He rarely works at night, never after midnight, but prefers the evening to the afternoon for literary production. He sometimes rewrites whole pages of his novels two or three times, but never makes a plan beforehand. He has the queer habit of making bread pellets while at work; that is, whenever he is absorbed in thought. He writes with facility and swiftness, devoting from three to four hours a day to literary labor.

Dr. Otto Franz Gensichen, German dramatist, poet, and essayist, always writes in the daytime, almost exclusively in the forenoon, from eight till twelve o'clock. He makes an exception in the case of lyrical poems, which, of course, must be written down whenever they occur to the mind. After his manuscript is done, he polishes it here and there, and then copies it; for while slowly transcribing he can most easily detect mistakes. While at work in the morning he smokes a mild cigar, which is, however, sometimes omitted. When writing, he likes to have as much light and silence about him as he can possibly attain. While the manuscript lies on the writing table, and the author is meditating on the subject in hand, he is in the habit of pacing up and down the room. At first he repeats the words aloud to test their euphonism and smoothness; he then commits the spoken words to paper. He can boast of himself that he has never written a line "invita Musa," without being fully inclined to composition. Sometimes he does not write for months, but when the proper mood takes possession of him, he is very industrious. Even then, however, he does most of his work before midday, and, exceptionally, from five till eight in the afternoon. As he is a bachelor and given up altogether to authorship, he is governed entirely by his moods.

Paul Burani, the brilliant Parisian journalist and dramatist, is forty years of age, married and father of one daughter,--Michelette,--owner of the house he lives in, and, altogether, the perfect type of a successful literarian. Before writing a play, he makes a very elaborate outline, which is developed afterward. Ordinarily he rewrites a play three times, but being both a ready and a rapid writer, the task is quickly accomplished. When compelled to stop writing in consequence of fatigue or a lack of interest, he takes up something else, promenades in his garden, or smokes a cigar. He is indifferent to noise, and can compose almost anywhere. The great number of books which he has written has given him the reputation of being one of the most productive authors of the times, but he does not write for more than five or six hours a day.

Ludwig Habicht, a German novelist, loves to write by the light of the sun, and invariably works in the daytime, never at night. When his manuscript is finished and corrected, he has it copied by a professional copyist, whereupon it goes to the compositor. Habicht prefers to write in the open air, and does not use a writing-desk. The duration of his working hours depends entirely upon his health and moods, but he never writes for more than four or five hours a day; and sometimes does not pen a line for months.

Formerly, when the world--that is to say, the German world--used to know Karl Stelter, the poet, as a merchant, he was in the habit of spending his leisure hours in the evening in the production of poetry, and, strange though it may seem, his best poems were made after a hard day's work. Now, since he has retired from business and is in prosperous circumstances, he versifies whenever and wherever he wants to, in the evening as well as in the daytime. He writes his poems with a lead pencil, and polishes them for weeks before they are published. He works with great ease, and is a ready improviser; but he never writes against his inclination.

Brander Matthews does his work between breakfast and lunch, as a rule; and works at night only occasionally. He makes elaborate notes, and then writes at white heat, revising at his leisure.

Andr?Theuriet, the Parisian novelist, makes an outline of his work first; he delineates each chapter of his novel, indicating the situations, personages, dialogues, and so on. Thereupon the novel soon assumes a definite form. Theuriet spends six hours a day at his writing-desk, but always in the morning. He does not believe in night work. In the afternoon he revises the work of the previous day. During working hours the author drinks two cups of tea and smokes one or two pipes of tobacco. Theuriet retires early in the evening, between ten and eleven o'clock, and rises in the morning at a quarter before six. This regular mode of life explains why the novelist is able to write so much, and is a key to the productiveness which has astonished his contemporaries.

Paul Lindau, another German novelist, critic, and journalist, dictates a great deal, sometimes without inclination, and sometimes after hasty lead-pencil sketches. When he writes himself only one manuscript is made. He incessantly smokes cigarettes while at work. Only when he has labored uninterruptedly a long time does he refresh himself with coffee, tea, wine, and water. As a rule, Lindau writes with ease. He declares that dictating tires him out more than if he should write himself, but by dictation he is enabled to do twice as much work as he could otherwise accomplish. Generally, he writes for from four to five hours a day, but sometimes he has spent ten or even eleven hours in literary work.

A. v. Winterfeld, the German humorist, devotes the day only to literary work. His original manuscript is committed to the press, for he never copies what he has written. He composes with great ease and swiftness, and spends four hours a day at the writing-desk.

Hector Malot, the Parisian novelist, makes an outline of his romances beforehand, faintly indicating all important incidents of his work. He does not take stimulating drinks, either when at work or when at rest; with him the work itself acts as a stimulant. He rises at five o'clock in the morning, and writes till eleven. After breakfast he takes a walk. At two o'clock in the afternoon he resumes work and keeps at it until seven o'clock in the evening; but he never composes at night. Nine months of the year are devoted to literary labor, but the remaining three months he spends in travel, study, and recreation.

Victorien Sardou, the dramatist, writes his play twice; first on little scraps of paper, then on foolscap. The first draft, when it is finished, is a maze of alterations and delineations.

Mezerai, the famous historian, used to study and write by candle-light, even at noonday in summer, and, as if there had been no sun in the world, always waited upon his company to the door with a candle in his hand.

"The method of Buckle, the historian," so says his biographer, "was chiefly remarkable for careful, systematic industry, and punctilious accuracy. His memory appeared to be almost faultless, yet he took as much precaution against failure as if he dared not trust it. He invariably read with "paper and pencil in his hand, making copious references for future consideration. How laboriously this system was acted upon can be appreciated only by those who have seen his note-books, in which the passages so marked during his reading were either copied or referred to under proper heads. Volume after volume was thus filled, everything being written with the same precise neatness that characterizes his manuscript for the press, and indexed with care, so that immediate reference might be made to any topic. But, carefully as these extracts and references were made, there was not a quotation in one of the copious notes that accompanied his work that was not verified by collation with the original from which it was taken."

Joaquin Miller says that he has always been so poor, or, rather, has had so many depending on his work, that he has "never been able to indulge the luxury of habits," and that he has worked in a sort of "catch-as-catch-can" way. Having been mostly on the wing since he began writing, he has done his work in all kinds of ways, and hours, and houses. However, now, since he has a little home, his life has become regulated. He rises at daylight, so as to save candles, and never works at night. After he has made and imbibed his coffee, he digs or pulls weeds, and cultivates his flowers, or works in some way about the greens, for an hour or so, and at length, when he feels compelled to literary work, and can no longer keep from it, he writes whatever he feels that he must set down; and then he writes only as long as he feels impelled. Holding, as he does, that all modern authors think too little and write too much, he never writes as long as he can keep from it. He looks forward with hope and pleasure to the day when he shall be able to stop writing entirely. As for stimulants, he never takes them. Yet he often smokes a cigar about the greens before beginning work. But he would be ill if he attempted to drink while writing. As for making an outline of his work, he generally jots down a lot of sketches or pictures, one each day; then he puts these together, and the play, poem, or novel is finished. He works for from three to five hours every day, then goes out till dinner time. He once lived in a rude log cabin, built on an eminence overlooking the city of Washington, D. C. There his latch-string was always out. He now lives near Oakland, Calif., not in one cabin, but in three, each as rude as that of any settler in the Sierras.

George Manville Fenn, during a period of some eighteen years, has tried a good many plans, with the result of settling down for the last twelve or fourteen years to one alone. He prefers the daytime decidedly for mental work, because the brain is fresh and vigorous from the rest of the past few hours, and because the work produced is lighter and better and can be sustained longer; and the writer is not exhausted when he leaves his table. Brilliant work has often been done at night; but when Fenn has made the trial he has found the results of a month's day-work better, and there has been more in quantity. He invariably makes an outline or skeleton of his work, and often with his story first in a dramatic form, which, he thinks, adds much to the vigor and effect of a tale. He is in the habit of using tobacco, but has never looked upon it as a stimulus, regarding it rather as a soothing aid to reflection. He dines early, so as to have the evenings free. The afternoon is spent in work, a visit to town, or a chat with friends; he takes tea early,--at six,--and afterward often writes for two or three hours. For years Mr. Fenn has been trying to solve this problem: Why can one write easily and fairly well one day, and have the next be almost a blank? After long study and much musing, he has come to the determination that he knows nothing whatever about it, and that the only thing to do is to lead as quiet and temperate a life as one can. Of course, the stimulated and excited brain will produce a few weird and powerful bits of work; but, judging from what Mr. Fenn has seen, the loaded mind soon breaks down.

VII.

Goethe, Dickens, Schiller, and Scott.

Goethe was a believer in the pleasant doctrine that the highest and freest work can be done under the healthiest conditions of fresh air, early hours, daylight, and temperance--which does not mean abstinence. He and Balzac are at precisely opposite pales in their method of working. Here is the account of Goethe's days at Weimar, according to G. H. Lewes: He rose at seven. Till eleven he worked without interruption. A cup of chocolate was then brought, and he worked on again till one. At two he dined. His appetite was immense. Even on the days when he complained of not being hungry, he ate much more than most men. He sat a long while over his wine, chatting gayly; for he never dined alone. He was fond of wine, and drank daily his two or three bottles. There was no dessert--Balzac's principal meal--nor coffee. Then he went to the theatre, where a glass of punch was brought to him at six, or else he received friends at home. By ten o'clock he was in bed, where he slept soundly. Like Thorwaldsen, he had a talent for sleeping.

No man of business or dictionary maker could make a more healthy arrangement of his hours. The five or six hours of regular morning work, which left the rest of the day open for society and recreation, the early habits, the full allowance of sleep, and the rational use of food are in glaring contrast to Balzac's short and broken slumbers, his night work, and his bodily starvation. Goethe differed from almost every other great poet in not doing his greatest work at a white heat; and not only so, but he differed also in constantly balancing his reasoning against his creative faculties. Those long mornings of early work were not always spent in the fever of creation. He was a physiologist, a botanist, a critic; and the longer he lived, the more of a savant he became, if not less of a poet. His imagination was most fertile before he settled down into these regular ways, but not before he settled down into a full appreciation of wine. Balzac would write the draft of a whole novel at a sitting, and then develop it on the margins of proofs, revises, and re-revises. Goethe acted as if while art is long, life were long also. Till the contrary is proved, we must consistently hold that Goethe was the philosopher before dinner-time, and the poet in the theatre, or during those long after-dinner hours over his two or three bottles of wine. That these later hours were often spent socially proves nothing, one way or the other. Some men need such active influences as their form of mental stimulus. Alfieri found, or made, his ideas while listening to music or galloping on horseback. Instances are common in every-day life of men who cannot think to good purpose when shut up in a room with a pen, and who find their best inspiration in wandering about the streets and hearing what they want in the rattle of cabs and the seething of life around them, like the scholar of Padua, whose conditions of work are given by Montaigne as a curiosity: "I lately found one of the most learned men in France studying in the corner of a room, cut off by a screen, surrounded by a lot of riotous servants. He told me--and Seneca says much the same himself--that he worked all the better for this uproar, as, if overpowered by noise, he was obliged to withdraw all the more closely into himself for contemplation, while the storm of voices drove his thoughts inward. When at Padua he had lodged so long over the clattering of the traffic and the tumult of the streets, that he had been trained not only to be indifferent to noise, but even to require it for the prosecution of his studies."

Goethe abominated smoking, though he was a German. Bayard Taylor says that he tolerated the use of the pipe by Schiller and his sovereign, Carl August, but otherwise he was very severe in denouncing it. Goethe himself somewhere says that "with tobacco, garlic, bed-bugs, and hypocrites he should wage perpetual war."

We learn from Mr. Forster that "method in everything was Dickens' peculiarity, and between breakfast and luncheon, with rare exceptions, was his time of work. But his daily walks were less of rule than of enjoyment and necessity. In the midst of his writing they were indispensable, and especially, as it has been shown, at night." When he had work on hand he walked all over the town furiously, and in all weathers, to the injury of his health; and his walks, be it observed, were frequently what Balzac's always were--at night; so that, in the matter of hours, he must be taken as having conformed in some important respects to Balzac's hygiene. Now, Goethe was also an essentially out-of-doors man by nature--not one to let his pen do his imagining for him. He was no slave of the ink-bottle, as some are, who cannot think without the feather of a goose in their hands, by way of a sometimes appropriate talisman. There is a well-known passage in one of the Roman elegies to the effect that inspiration is to be sought more directly than within the four walls of a study, and that the rhythm of the hexameter is not best drummed with the fingers on a wooden table; and if it is true, as the author tells, that "youth is drunkenness without wine," it seems to follow, according to his experience, that those two or three bottles of wine are not altogether needless as an aid to inspiration when youth is gone by.

Schiller could never leave off talking about his poetical projects, and thus he discussed with Goethe all his best pieces, scene after scene. On the other hand, it was contrary to Goethe's nature, as he told Eckermann, to talk over his poetic plans with anybody--even with Schiller. He carried everything about with him in silence, and usually nothing of what he was doing was known to any one until the whole was completed.

Sir Walter Scott was one of the most industrious of writers. He rose early, and accomplished a good day's literary work before half the world was out of bed. Even when he was busiest, he seldom worked as late as noon. His romances were composed with amazing rapidity; and it is an astonishing fact, that in less than two weeks after his bankruptcy Scott wrote an entire volume of "Woodstock." His literary labors yielded him $50,000 a year. Two thousand copies of "The Lady of the Lake" were sold within a few months.

Many of the more energetic descriptions in "Marmion," and particularly that of the battle of Flodden, were struck off, according to Mr. Skene's account, while Scott was out with his cavalry, in the autumn of 1807. In the intervals of drilling, we are told, Scott used to delight "in walking his powerful black steed up and down by himself upon the Portobello sands, within the beating of the surge; and now and then you would see him plunge in his spurs, and go off as if at the charge, with the spray dashing about him. As we rode back to Musselburgh, he often came and placed himself beside me, to repeat the verses that he had been composing during these pauses of our exercise."

In after years, Mr. Cadell, then a guest at Abbotsford, observing how his host was harassed by lion-hunters, and what a number of hours he spent daily in the company of his work-people, expressed his wonder that Scott should ever be able to work at all while in the country. "Oh," said Sir Walter, "I lie simmering over things for an hour or so before I get up; and there's the time I'm dressing to overhaul my half-sleeping, half-waking projet de chapitre, and when I get the paper before me, it commonly runs off pretty easily. Besides, I often take a doze in the plantations, and while Tom [Purdie] marks out a dyke or a drain as I have directed, one's fancy may be running its ain rigs in some other world."

By far the greater portion of "The Bride of Lammermoor," the whole of "The Legend of Montrose," and almost the whole of "Ivanhoe" were dictated under the terrible stimulus of physical pain, which wrung groans from the author between the words. The very two novels wherein the creative power of the arch-master of romance shows itself most strongly were composed in the midst of literal birth-throes. Laidlaw would often beseech Sir Walter affectionately to stop dictating, when his audible suffering filled every pause. It was then he made that grimmest of all bad puns: "Nay, Willie," addressing Laidlaw, who wrote for him and implored him to rest, "only see that the doors are fast. I would fain keep all the cry, as well as all the wool, to ourselves; but as to giving over work, that can be done only when I am in woollen." John Ballantyne, his other faithful amanuensis, after the first day, took care to have always a dozen of pens made before he seated himself opposite the sofa on which Scott lay, the sufferer usually continuing his sentence in the same breath, though he often turned himself on his pillow with a groan of anguish. "But when a dialogue of peculiar animation was in progress, spirit seemed to triumph altogether over matter: he arose from his couch and walked up and down the room, raising and lowering his voice, and, as it were, acting the parts."

In this last particular we are reminded of the celebrated Russian author, Gogol, whose practice it is said to have been in composing a dialogue to recite all the different speeches in character before committing them to paper, to assure himself of their being in complete consonance with what the character and situation required.

So far from affording any argument to the contrary, the history of the years during which Sir Walter's hand was losing its cunning seems to illustrate the penalty of trying to reconcile two irreconcilable things--the exercise of the imagination to its fullest extent, and the observance of conditions that are too healthy to nourish a fever. Apropos of his review of Ritson's "Caledonian Annals," he himself says: "No one that has not labored as I have done on imaginary topics can judge of the comfort afforded by walking on all-fours, and being grave and dull." There spoke the man who habitually, and without artificial help, drew upon his imagination at the hours when instinct has told others they should be employing, not their fancy, but their reason. The privilege of being healthily dull before breakfast must have been an intense relief to one who compelled himself to do unhealthy or abnormal work without the congenial help of abnormal conditions. Herder, in like manner, is accused by De Quincey, in direct terms, of having broken down prematurely because he "led a life of most exemplary temperance. Surely, if he had been a drunkard or an opium-eater, he might have contrived to weather the point of sixty years." This is putting things pretty strongly; but it is said of a man of great imaginative power by a man of great imaginative power, and may, therefore, be taken as the opinion of an expert, all the more honest because he is prejudiced. A need must be strongly felt to be expressed with such daring contempt for popular axioms.

The true working-life of Scott, who helped nature by no artificial means, lasted for no more than twelve years, from the publication of "Waverley" until the year in which his genius was put into harness; so that, of the two men, Scott and Balzac, who both began a literary life at nearly the same age, and were both remarkable for splendid constitutions, the man who lived abnormally surpassed the man who lived healthily by fully eight years of good work, and kept his imagination in full vigor to the end.

It is amusing to read Sir Walter's candid avowal, when beginning the third volume of "Woodstock," that he "had not the slightest idea how the story was to be wound up to a catastrophe." He declares he never could lay down a plan--or that, if he had laid one down, he never could stick to it. "I tried only to make that which I was writing diverting and interesting, leaving the rest to fate. This habnab at a venture is a perilous style, I grant, but I cannot help it."

VIII.

Burning Midnight Oil.

That night, and not morning, is most appropriate to imaginative work is supported by a general consent among those who have followed instinct in this matter. Upon this question, which can scarcely be called vexed, Charles Lamb is the classical authority: "No true poem ever owed its birth to the sun's light. The mild, internal light, that reveals the fine shapings of poetry, like fires on the domestic hearth, goes out in the sunshine. Milton's 'Morning Hymn in Paradise,' we would hold a good wager, was penned at midnight, and Taylor's rich description of a sunrise smells decidedly of a taper." "This view of evening and candle-light," to quote his commentator, De Quincey, once more, "as involved in the full delight of literature," may seem no more than a pleasant extravaganza, and no doubt it is in the nature of such gayeties to travel a little into exaggeration; but substantially it is certain that Lamb's sincere feelings pointed habitually in the direction here indicated. His literary studies, whether taking the color of tasks or diversions, courted the aid of evening, which, by means of physical weariness, produces a more luxurious state of repose than belongs to the labor hours of day; they courted the aid of lamp-light, which, as Lord Bacon remarked, "gives a gorgeousness to human pomps and pleasures, such as would be vainly sought from the homeliness of day-light." Those words, "physical weariness," if they do not contain the whole philosophy of the matter, are very near it, and are, at all events, more to the point than the quotation from Lord Bacon. They almost exactly define that unnatural condition of the body which, on other grounds, appears to be proper to the unnatural exercise of the mind. It will be remembered that Balzac recommended the night for the artist's work, the day for the author's drudgery. Southey, who knew as well as anybody who ever put pen to paper how to work, and how to get the best and the most out of himself, and who pursued the same daily routine through his whole literary life, performed his tasks in the following order: From breakfast till dinner, history, transcription for the press, and, in general, all the work that Scott calls "walking on all-fours." From dinner till tea, reading, letter-writing, the newspapers, and frequently a siesta--he, also, was a heroic sleeper, and slept whenever he had the chance. After tea, poetry, or whatever else his fancy chose--whatever work called upon the creative power. It is true that he went to bed regularly at half-past ten, so that his actual consumption of midnight oil was not extravagant. But such of it as he did consume served as a stimulant for the purely imaginative part of his work, when the labor that required no stimulant was over and done.

Blake was a painter by day and a poet by night; he often got out of bed at midnight and wrote for hours, following by instinct the deliberate practice of less impulsive workers.

Schiller evolved his finest plays in a summer-house, which he built for himself, with a single chamber, on the top of an acclivity near Jena, commanding a beautiful prospect of the valley of the Saal and the fir mountains of the neighboring forest. On sitting down to his desk at night, says During, he was wont to keep some strong coffee or wine chocolate, but more frequently a flask of old Rhenish or champagne, standing by him: often the neighbors would hear him earnestly declaiming in the silence of the night, and he might be seen walking swiftly to and fro in his chamber, then suddenly throwing himself down into his chair and writing, drinking at intervals from the glass that stood near him. In winter he continued at his desk till four, or even five, o'clock in the morning; in summer, till toward three. The "pernicious expedient of stimulants" served only to waste the more speedily and surely, as Mr. Carlyle says, his already wasted fund of physical strength. Schiller used an artificial stimulus altogether peculiar to himself: he found it impossible, according to the well-known anecdote, to work except in a room filled with the scent of rotten apples, which he kept in a drawer of his writing-table, in order to keep up his necessary mental atmosphere.

In the park at Weimar we have other glimpses of Schiller; frequently he was to be seen there, wandering among the groves and remote avenues,--for he loved solitary walks,--with a note-book in his hand; now loitering along, now moving rapidly on; "if any one appeared in sight, he would dart into another alley, that his dream might not be broken." In Joerden's Lexicon we read that whatever Schiller intended to write, he first composed in his head, before putting down a line of it on paper; and he used to call a work "ready" so soon as its existence in his spirit was complete: hence, there were often reports current of his having finished such and such a work, when, in the common sense, it was not even begun.

Lord Byron was a late riser. He often saw the sun rise before he went to bed. In his journals we frequently find such entries as these: "Got up at two P. M., spent the morning," etc. He always wrote at night. While he was the most brilliant star in London society, he was in the habit of returning from balls, routs, the theatre, and opera, and then writing for two or three hours before going to bed. In this way "The Corsair," "Lara," "The Giaour," and "The Siege of Corinth" were composed. Byron affords an illustration of a tendency to put himself out of working condition in order to work the better. "At Disdati," says Moore, "his life was passed in the same regular round of habits into which he naturally fell." These habits included very late hours and semi-starvation, the excessive smoking of cigars and chewing of tobacco, and the drinking of green tea, without milk or sugar, in the evening. Like Balzac, Byron avoided meat and wine, and so gave less natural brain-food room for active play.

The experience of P. K. Rosegger, the greatest novelist of Styria, whose popular works are read not only in the palace, but also in the hut, is contrary to that of most writers; he finds that with him lamp-light and night-work are most conducive to literary fertility, and that he can work with greater ease on dark, gloomy days than in fine weather. His manuscripts are generally committed to the press as they were originally composed, except for additions that fill the margins which the author leaves for that purpose when writing. Poetry comes to him spontaneously when he takes his exercise in the field or garden, so that all he has to do when he gets home is to write it down; but he can compose prose only at the writing-desk. After a rest of several days he writes with great ease and velocity; in fact, writing is a necessity to him. On the average, he writes three hours a day. He is often forced to write while disinclined, to provide for the maintenance of a large family.

George Parsons Lathrop thus speaks of the habits of work of Dr. William A. Hammond, one of the more recent additions to our novel-writers: "Dr. Hammond's habits of work are something which should interest all brain laborers. At a moderately early hour in the morning he seats himself in his consulting-room to receive patients, and he remains indoors until two in the afternoon. Then he drives out and walks. On certain days he has medical lectures to deliver. His spare time in the afternoon is devoted to taking the air, reading, or diverting himself. After dinner and any social recreation that may be in hand he sits down at his desk again by ten or eleven o'clock, and writes until two in the morning. 'I do it,' he says, 'because I like it. It amuses and refreshes me.' How he manages to endure this constant sitting up is something of a marvel, considering that so much of his energies must be consumed by professional work. He seems to be always at leisure and unharassed, and lives comfortably, not denying himself a reasonable portion of stimulants and tobacco."

IX.

Literary Partnership.

Literary partnerships are common in France, but in England they are confined almost exclusively to dramatists. The one well-known exception was that of Messrs. Besant and Rice. Mr. Rice's partnership with Mr. Besant began in 1871, and ended with the death of Mr. Rice. "It arose," explains Mr. Besant, "out of some slight articles which I contributed to his magazine, and began with the novel called 'Ready-Money Mortiboy.' Of this eleven years' fellowship and intimate, almost daily, intercourse, I can say only that it was carried on throughout without a single shadow of dispute or difference. James Rice was eminently a large-minded man, and things which might have proved great rocks of offence to some, he knew how to treat as the trifles they generally are."

In France, the best example of literary partnership is found in that of M. Erckmann and M. Chatrian. How these men worked in concert has been described by the author of "Men of the Third Republic." "M. Chatrian is credited with being the more imaginative of the two. The first outlines of the plots are generally his, as also the love scenes, and all the descriptions of Phalsbourg and the country around. M. Erckmann puts in the political reflections, furnishes the soldier types, and elaborates those plain speeches which fit so quaintly, but well, into the mouths of his honest peasants, sergeants, watchmakers, and schoolmasters. A clever critic remarked that Erckmann-Chatrian's characters are always hungry and eating. The blame, if any, must lie on M. Chatrian's shoulders; to his fancy belong the steaming tureens of soup, the dishes of browned sausages and sauer-kraut, and the mounds of flowery potatoes, bursting plethorically through their skins. All that M. Erckmann adds is the black coffee, of which he insists, with some energy, on being a connoisseur. Habitually the co-authors meet to sketch out their plots and talk them over amid much tobacco smoking. Then, when the story has taken clear shape in their minds, one or the other of the pair writes the first chapter, leaving blanks for the dialogues or descriptions which are best suited to the competency of the other. Every chapter thus passes through both writers' hands, is revised, recopied, and, as occasion requires, either shortened or lengthened in the process. When the whole book is written, both authors revise it again, and always with a view to curtailment. Novelists who dash off six volumes of diluted fiction in a year, and affect to think naught of the feat, would grow pensive at seeing the labor bestowed by MM. Erckmann and Chatrian on the least of their works, as well as their patient research in assuring themselves that their historical episodes are correct, and their descriptions of existing localities true to nature. But this careful industry will have its reward, for the novels of MM. Erckmann and Chatrian will live. The signs of vitality were discovered in them as soon as the two authors, nerved by their first success, settled down and produced one tale after another, all too slowly for the public demand. 'The Story of a Conscript,' 'Waterloo,' 'The History of a Man of the People,' and, above all,

'The History of a Peasant,' were read with wonder as well as interest."

X.

Anonymity in Authorship.

The question of the authorship of certain popular works has given rise to a great deal of speculation. A few years ago, it will be remembered, we were puzzling our brains to discover the name of the author of "The Breadwinners." Among other stinging charges against him, to induce him to break the silence, was the fling that it was a base and craven thing to publish a book anonymously. "My motive in withholding my name is simple enough," said the unknown author to his furious critics. "I am engaged in business in which my standing would be seriously compromised were it known that I had written a novel. I am sure that my practical efficiency is not lessened by this act, but I am equally sure that I could never recover from the injury it would occasion me if known among my own colleagues. For that positive reason, and for the negative one that I do not care for publicity, I resolved to keep the knowledge of my little venture in authorship restricted to as small a circle as possible. Only two persons besides myself know who wrote 'The Breadwinners.'"

A far more serious dispute followed the publication of the "Vestiges of Creation," forty years ago. The theologians of Scotland were wild with rage at the audacity of the author, who would have been torn to pieces almost had he been discovered. In scientific circles Robert Chambers was credited with the authorship; and Henri Grille seems to have had no doubt upon the matter. In "Leaves from the Diary of Henri Grille" there is an entry under the date December 28, 1847, as follows: "I have been reading a novel called 'Jane Eyre,' which is just now making a great sensation, and which absorbed and interested me more than any novel I can recollect having read. The author is unknown. Mrs. Butler,--Miss Fannie Kemble,--who is greatly struck by the talent of the book, fancies it is written by Chambers, who is the author of the 'Vestiges of Creation,' because she thinks that whoever wrote it must, from its language, be a Scotchman, and from its sentiments be a Unitarian; and Chambers, besides answering to all these peculiarities, has an intimate friend who believes in supernatural agencies, such as are described in the last volume of the book." Thackeray also had the credit of the work.

Nobody knew Charlotte Bront? but she was unable to keep her secret very long. The late R. H. Horne was present at that first dinner party given by George Smith, the publisher, when Currer Bell, then in the first flush of her fame, made her earliest appearance in a London dining-room. She was anxious to preserve the anonymity of her literary character, and was introduced by her true name. Horne, however, who sat next to her, was so fortunate as to discover her identity. Just previously he had sent to the new author, under cover of her publisher, a copy of his "Orion." In an unguarded moment, Charlotte Bront?turned to him and said:--

"I was so much obliged to you, Mr. Horne, for sending me your--" But she checked herself with an inward start, having thus betrayed her Currer Bell secret, by identifying herself with the author of "Jane Eyre."

"Ah, Miss Bront?" whispered the innocent cause of the misfortune, "you would never do for treasons and stratagems!"

The late John Blackwood corresponded with George Eliot for some time before he knew that she was a woman. He called her "Dear George," he says, and often used expressions which a man commonly uses only to a man. After he found out who "Dear George" was, he was naturally a little anxious to recall some of the expressions he had used. Charles Dickens, however, detected what escaped the observation of most people. Writing to a correspondent in January, 1858, he said: "Will you, by such roundabout ways and methods as may present themselves, convey this note of thanks to the author of 'Scenes of Clerical Life,' whose two first stories I can never say enough of, I think them so truly admirable. But, if those two volumes, or a part of them, were not written by a woman, then shall I begin to believe that I am a woman myself."

XI.

System in Novel Writing.

Anthony Trollope was the most systematic of all the English novelists. Sitting down at his desk, he would take out his watch and time himself. His system is well known, but a singular explanation of his fertility may be quoted: "When I have commenced a new book," he says, "I have always prepared a diary divided into weeks, and carried it on for the period which I have allowed myself for the completion of the work. In this I have entered day by day the number of pages I have written, so that if at any time I have slipped into idleness for a day or two, the record of that idleness has been there staring me in the face and demanding of me increased labor, so that the deficiency might be supplied. According to the circumstances of the time, whether any other business might be then heavy or light, or whether the book which I was writing was or was not wanted with speed, I have allotted myself so many pages a week. The average number has been about forty. It has been placed as low as twenty and has risen to one hundred and twelve. And as a page is an ambiguous term, my page has been made to contain two hundred and fifty words, and as words, if not watched, will have a tendency to straggle, I have had every word counted as I went."

Under the title of "A Walk in a Wood," Anthony Trollope thus describes his method of plot-making and the difficulty the novelist experiences in making the "tricksy Ariel" of the imagination do his bidding: "I have to confess that my incidents are fabricated to fit my story as it goes on, and not my story to fit my incidents. I wrote a novel once in which a lady forged a will, but I had not myself decided that she had forged it till the chapter before that in which she confesses her guilt. In another a lady is made to steal her own diamonds, a grand tour de force, as I thought; but the brilliant idea struck me only when I was writing the page in which the theft is described. I once heard an unknown critic abuse my workmanship because a certain lady had been made to appear too frequently in my pages. I went home and killed her immediately. I say this to show that the process of thinking to which I am alluding has not generally been applied to any great effort of construction. It has expended itself on the minute ramifications of tale-telling: how this young lady should be made to behave herself with that young gentleman; how this mother or that father would be affected by the ill conduct or the good of a son or a daughter; how these words or those other would be most appropriate or true to nature if used on some special occasion. Such plottings as these with a fabricator of fiction are infinite in number, but not one of them can be done fitly without thinking. My little effort will miss its wished-for result unless I be true to nature; and to be true to nature I must think what nature would produce. Where shall I go to find my thoughts with the greatest ease and most perfect freedom?

"I have found that I can best command my thoughts on foot, and can do so with the most perfect mastery when wandering through a wood. To be alone is, of course, essential. Companionship requires conversation, for which, indeed, the spot is most fit; but conversation is not now the object in view. I have found it best even to reject the society of a dog, who, if he be a dog of manners, will make some attempt at talking; and though he should be silent, the sight of him provokes words and caresses and sport. It is best to be away from cottages, away from children, away as far as may be from chance wanderers. So much easier is it to speak than to think, that any slightest temptation suffices to carry away the idler from the harder to the lighter work. An old woman with a bundle of sticks becomes an agreeable companion, or a little girl picking wild fruit. Even when quite alone, when all the surroundings seem to be fitted for thought, the thinker will still find a difficulty in thinking. It is not that the mind is inactive, but that it will run exactly whither it is not bidden to go. With subtle ingenuity, it will find for itself little easy tasks, instead of setting itself down on that which it is its duty to do at once. With me, I own, it is so weak as to fly back to things already done, which require no more thinking, which are, perhaps, unworthy of a place even in the memory, and to revel in the ease of contemplating that which has been accomplished, rather than to struggle for further performance. My eyes, which should become moist with the troubles of the embryo heroine, shed tears as they call to mind the early sorrow of Mr. ----, who was married and made happy many years ago. Then, when it comes to this, a great effort becomes necessary, or that day will for me have no results. It is so easy to lose an hour in maundering over the past, and to waste the good things which have been provided in remembering instead of creating!

"But a word about the nature of the wood! It is not always easy to find a wood, and sometimes when you have got it, it is but a muddy, plashy, rough-hewn congregation of ill-grown trees,--a thicket rather than a wood,--in which even contemplation is difficult, and thinking is out of the question. He who has devoted himself to wandering in woods will know at the first glance whether the place will suit his purpose. A crowded undergrowth of hazel, thorn, birch, and elder, with merely a track through it, will by no means serve the occasion. The trees around you should be big and noble. There should be grass at your feet. There should be space for the felled or fallen princes of the forest. A roadway with the sign of wheels that have passed long since will be an advantage, so long as the branches above your head shall meet or seem to meet each other. I will not say that the ground should not be level, lest by creating difficulties I shall seem to show that the fitting spot may be too difficult to be found; but, no doubt, it will be an assistance in the work to be done if occasionally you can look down on the tops of the trees as you descend, and again look up to them as with increasing height they rise high above your head. And it should be a wood--perhaps a forest--rather than a skirting of timber. You should feel that, if not lost, you are losable. To have trees around you is not enough, unless you have many. You must have a feeling as of Adam in the garden. There must be a confirmed assurance in your mind that you have got out of the conventional into the natural, which will not establish itself unless there be a consciousness of distance between you and the next ploughed field. If possible, you should not know the east from the west; or, if so, only by the setting of the sun. You should recognize the direction in which you must return simply by the fall of water.

"But where shall the wood be found? Such woodlands there are still in England, though, alas! they are becoming rarer every year. Profit from the timber merchant or dealer in fire-wood is looked to; or else, as is more probable, drives are cut broad and straight, like spokes of a wheel radiating to a nave or centre, good only for the purposes of the slayer of multitudinous pheasants. I will not say that a wood prepared, not as the home, but the slaughter-ground, of game, is altogether inefficient for our purpose. I have used such, even when the sound of the guns has been near enough to warn me to turn my steps to the right or to the left. The scents are pleasant even in winter; the trees are there, and sometimes even yet the delightful feeling may be encountered that the track on which you are walking leads to some far-off, vague destination, in reaching which there may be much of delight, because it will be new;--something also of peril, because it will be distant. But the wood, if possible, should seem to be purposeless. It should have no evident consciousness of being there, either for game or fagots. The felled trunk on which you sit should seem to have been selected for some accidental purpose of house-building, as if a neighbor had searched for what was wanting and had found it. No idea should be engendered that it was let out at so much an acre to a contractor, who would cut the trees in order and sell them in the next market. The mind should conceive that this wood never had been planted by hands, but had come there from the direct beneficence of the Creator--as the first woods did come, before man had been taught to recreate them systematically, and as some still remain to us, so much more lovely in their wildness than when reduced to rows and quincunxes, and made to accommodate themselves to laws of economy and order.

"They will not come at once, those thoughts which are so anxiously expected; and in the process of coming they are apt to be troublesome, full of tricks, and almost traitorous. They must be imprisoned or bound with thongs when they come, as was Proteus when Ulysses caught him amidst his sea-calves,--as was done with some of the fairies of old, who would, indeed, do their beneficent work, but only under compulsion. It may be that your spirit should on an occasion be as obedient as Ariel; but that will not be often. He will run backward,--as it were downhill,--because it is so easy, instead of upward and onward. He will turn to the right and to the left, making a show of doing fine work, only not the work that is demanded of him that day. He will skip hither and thither with pleasant, bright gambols, but will not put his shoulder to the wheel, his neck to the collar, his hand to the plough. Has my reader ever driven a pig to market? The pig will travel on freely, but will always take the wrong turning; and then, when stopped for the tenth time, will head backward and try to run between your legs So it is with the tricksy Ariel,--that Ariel which every man owns, though so many of us fail to use him for much purpose; which but few of us have subjected to such discipline as Prospero had used before he had brought his servant to do his bidding at the slightest word.

"But at last I feel that I have him, perhaps by the tail, as the Irishman drives his pig. When I have got him I have to be careful that he shall not escape me till that job of work be done. Gradually, as I walk or stop, as I seat myself on a bank or lean against a tree, perhaps as I hurry on waving my stick above my head, till, with my quick motion, the sweatdrops come out upon my brow, the scene forms itself for me. I see, or fancy that I see, what will be fitting, what will be true, how far virtue may be made to go without walking upon stilts, what wickedness may do without breaking the link which binds it to humanity, how low ignorance may grovel, how high knowledge may soar, what the writer may teach without repelling by severity, how he may amuse without descending to buffoonery; and then the limits of pathos are searched and words are weighed which shall suit, but do no more than suit, the greatness or the smallness of the occasion. We, who are slight, may not attempt lofty things, or make ridiculous with our little fables the doings of the gods. But for that which we do there are appropriate terms and boundaries which may be reached, but not surpassed. All this has to be thought of and decided upon in reference to those little plottings of which I have spoken, each of which has to be made the receptacle of pathos or of humor, of honor or of truth, as far as the thinker may be able to furnish them. He has to see, above all things, that in his attempts he shall not sin against nature; that in striving to touch the feelings he shall not excite ridicule; that in seeking for humor he does not miss his point; that in quest of honor and truth he does not become bombastic and straitlaced. A clergyman in his pulpit may advocate an altitude of virtue fitted to a millennium here or to a heaven hereafter; nay, from the nature of his profession, he must do so. The poet, too, may soar as high as he will, and if words suffice to him, he need never fear to fail because his ideas are too lofty. But he who tells tales in prose can hardly hope to be effective as a teacher, unless he binds himself by the circumstances of the world which he finds around him. Honor and truth there should be, and pathos and humor, but he should so constrain them that they shall not seem to mount into nature beyond the ordinary habitations of men and women.

"Such rules as to construction have probably been long known to him. It is not for them he is seeking as he is roaming listlessly or walking rapidly through the trees. They have come to him from much observation, from the writings of others, from that which we call study, in which imagination has but little immediate concern. It is the fitting of the rules to the characters which he has created, the filling in with living touches and true colors those daubs and blotches on his canvas which have been easily scribbled with a rough hand, that the true work consists. It is here that he requires that his fancy should be undisturbed, that the trees should overshadow him, that the birds should comfort him, that the green and yellow mosses should be in unison with him, that the very air should be good to him. The rules are there fixed,--fixed as far as his judgment can fix them,--and are no longer a difficulty to him. The first coarse outlines of his story he has found to be a matter almost indifferent to him. It is with these little plottings that he has to contend. It is for them that he must catch his Ariel and bind him fast, but yet so bind him that not a thread shall touch the easy action of his wings. Every little scene must be arranged so that--if it may be possible--the proper words may be spoken and the fitting effect produced.

"Alas! with all these struggles, when the wood has been found, when all external things are propitious, when the very heavens have lent their aid, it is so often that it is impossible! It is not only that your Ariel is untrained, but that the special Ariel which you may chance to own is no better than a rustic hobgoblin or a pease-blossom, or mustard seed at the best. You cannot get the pace of the racehorse from a farmyard colt, train him as you will. How often is one prompted to fling one's self down in despair, and, weeping between the branches, to declare that it is not that the thoughts will wander, it is not that the mind is treacherous! That which it can do, it will do; but the pace required from it should be fitted only for the farmyard. Nevertheless, before all be given up, let a walk in the wood be tried."

Much has been said about the quality of Mr. Trollope's work. There seems a consensus of opinion that it degenerated. "Mr. Trollope," says Mr. Freeman, "had certainly gone far to write himself out. His later work is far from being so good as his earlier. But, after all, his worst work is better than a great many other people's best; and considering the way in which it was done, it is wonderful that it was done at all. I, myself, know what fixed hours of work are, and their value; but I could not undertake to write about William Rufus or Appius Claudius up to a certain moment on the clock, and to stop at that moment. I suppose it was from his habits of official business that Mr. Trollope learned to do it, and every man undoubtedly knows best how to do his own work. Still, it is strange that works of imagination did not suffer by such a way of doing."

James Payn said that Trollope injured his reputation by publishing his methods of writing. Likewise, the Daily News, in referring to Alphonse Daudet's history of his own novels, doubted whether he acted wisely. As the editor said, "An effect of almost too elaborate art, a feeling that we are looking at a mosaic painfully made up of little pieces picked out of real life and fitted together, has often been present to the consciousness of M. Daudet's readers. That feeling is justified by his description of his creative efforts."

M. Daudet's earlier works were light and humorous, like "Tartarin," or they were idyllic and full of Provencial scenery, the nature and the nightingales of M. Daudet's birthplace, the south. One night at the theatre, when watching the splendid failure of an idyllic Provencial sort of play, M. Daudet made up his mind that he must give the public sterner stuff, and describe the familiar Parisian scenery of streets and quais. This wise determination was the origin of his novels, "Jack," "Fromont jeune et Risler ain?" and the rest. Up to that time, M. Daudet, M. Zola, M. Flaubert, and the brothers Goncourt had all been more or less unpopular authors. It is not long since they had a little club of the unsuccessful, and M. Daudet was the first of the company who began to blossom out into numerous editions.

M. Daudet's secret as a novelist, as far as the secret is communicable, seems to be his wonderfully close study of actual life and his unscrupulousness in reproducing its details almost without disguise. He frankly confesses that not only the characters in his political novels, but those in his other works, are drawn straight from living persons. The scenery is all sketched from nature, M. Daudet describing the vast factories with which he was familiar when, at the age of sixteen, he began to earn his own living, or the interiors to which he was admitted by virtue of his position under a great man of the late imperial administration. Places about which he did not know much, and which needed to be introduced into his tales, M. Daudet visited with his note-book.

M. Daudet's mode of work is, first, to see his plot and main incidents clearly, to arrive at a full understanding of his characters, then to map out his chapters, and then, he says, his fingers tingle to be at work. He writes rapidly, handing each wet slip of paper to Madame Daudet for criticism and approval. There is no such sound criticism, he says, as that of this helpful collaborator, who withal is "so little a woman of letters."

When a number of chapters are finished M. Daudet finds it well to begin publishing his novel in a journal. Thus he is obliged to finish within a certain date; he cannot go back to make alterations; he cannot afford time to write a page a dozen times over, as a conscientious artist often wishes to do.

XII.

Traits of Musical Composers.

A long chapter of instances might be penned on the habits of work of musical composers; such as Gluck's habit of betaking himself with his harpsichord on a fine day into some grassy field, where the ideas came to him as fast again as within doors.

Handel, on the contrary, claims to have been inspired for his grandest compositions by the murmurous din of mighty London,--far from mighty as the London of George the Second may seem to those with whom the nineteenth century is waning.

Sarti composed best in the sombre shadows of a dimly-lighted room.

The Monsieur Le Mare commemorated in Rousseau's autobiography typified a numerous section in his constant recourse, en travaillant dans son cabinet, to a bottle, which was replenished as often as emptied, and that was too often by a great deal. His servant, in preparing the room for him, would no more have thought of omitting son pot et son verre than his ruled paper, ink, pens, and violoncello; and one serving did for these,--not so for the drink.

The learned artist Haydn could not work except in court-dress, and used to declare that, if, when he sat down to his instrument, he had forgotten to put on a certain ring, he could not summon a single idea. How he managed to summon ideas before Frederick II. had given him the said ring we are not informed.

Charles Dibdin's method of composition, or, rather, the absence of it, is illustrated in the story of his lamenting his lack of a new subject while under the hair-dresser's hand in a cloud of powder, at his rooms in the Strand, preparing for his night's "entertainment." The friend who was with him suggested various topics, but all of a sudden the jar of a ladder sounded against the lamp-iron, and Dibdin exclaimed, "The lamp-lighter, a good notion," and at once began humming and fingering on his knee. As soon as his head was dressed he stepped to the piano, finished off both music and words, and that very night sang "Jolly Dick, the Lamplighter," at the theatre, nor could he, we are assured on critical authority, well have made a greater hit if the song had been the deliberate work of two authors--one of the words, another of the air--and had taken weeks to finish it, and been elaborated in studious leisure instead of the distraction of dressing-room din.

XIII.

The Hygiene of Writing.

Edward Everett Hale gives the following description of his mode of life, which at the same time is full of advice to authors in general:--

"The business of health for a literary man seems to me to depend largely upon sleep. He should have enough sleep, and should sleep well. He should avoid whatever injures sleep.

"This means that the brain should not be excited or even worked hard for six hours before bedtime. Young men can disregard this rule, and do; but as one grows older he finds it wiser to throw his work upon morning hours. If he can spend the afternoon, or even the evening, in the open air, his chances of sleep are better. The evening occupation, according to me, should be light and pleasant, as music, a novel, reading aloud, conversation, the theatre, or watching the stars from the piazza. Of course, different men make and need different rules. I take nine hours for sleep in every twenty-four, and do not object to ten.

"I accepted very early in life Bulwer's estimate that three hours a day is as large an average of desk work as a man of letters should try for. I have, in old newspaper days, written for twelve consecutive hours; but this is only a tour de force, and in the long run you waste strength if you do not hold every day quite closely to the average.

"As men live, with the telegraph and the telephone interrupting when they choose, and this fool and that coming in when they choose to say, 'I do not want to interrupt you; I will only take a moment,' the great difficulty is to hold your three hours without a break. If a man has broken my mirror, I do not thank him for leaving the pieces next each other; he has spoiled it, and he may carry them ten miles apart if he chooses. So, if a fool comes in and breaks my time in two, he may stay if he wants to; he is none the less a fool. What I want for work is unbroken time. This is best secured early in the morning.

"I dislike early rising as much as any man, nor do I believe there is any moral merit in it, as the children's books pretend; but to secure an unbroken hour, or even less, I like to be at my desk before breakfast. As long before as possible I have a cup of coffee and a soda biscuit brought me there, and in the thirty to sixty minutes which follow before breakfast, I like to start the work of the day. If you rise at a quarter past six, there will be comparatively few map pedlers, or book agents, or secretaries of charities, or jailbirds, who will call before eight. The hour from 6.30 to 7.30 is that of which you are most sure. Even the mother-in-law or the mother of your wife's sister's husband does not come then to say that she should like some light work with a large salary as matron in an institution where there is nothing to do.

"I believe in breakfast very thoroughly, and in having a good breakfast. I have lived in Paris a month at a time and detest the French practice of substituting for breakfast a cup of coffee, with or without an egg. Breakfast is a meal at which much time may be spent with great advantage. People are not apt to come to it too regularly, and you may profit by the intermission to read your newspaper and lecture on its contents. There's no harm in spending an hour at the table.

"After breakfast do not go to work for an hour. Walk out in the garden, lie on your back on a sofa and read, in general, 'loaf' for that hour, and bid the servant keep out everybody who rings the bell, and work steadily till your day's stint is done. If you have had half an hour before breakfast, you can make two hours and a half now.

"It is just so much help if you have a good amanuensis; none, if you have a poor one. The amanuensis should have enough else to do, but be at liberty to attend to you when you need. Write as long as you feel like writing; the moment you do not feel like it, give him the pen and walk up and down the room dictating. There are those who say that they can tell the difference between dictated work and work written by the author. I do not believe them. I will give a share in the Combination Protoxide Silver Mine of Grey's Gulch to anybody who will divide this article correctly between the parts which I dictated and those which are written with my own red right hand.

"Stick to your stint till it is done. If Philistines come in, as they will in a finite world, deduct the time which they have stolen from you and go on so much longer with your work till you have done what you set out to do.

"When you have finished the stint, stop. Do not be tempted to go on because you are in good spirits for work. There is no use in making ready to be tired to-morrow. You may go out of doors now, you may read, you may in whatever way get light and life for the next day. Indeed, if you will remember that the first necessity for literary work is that you have something ready to say before you begin, you will remember something which most authors have thoroughly forgotten or never knew.

"This business of writing is the most exhausting known to men. You should, therefore, steadily feed the machine with fuel. I find it a good habit to have standing on the stove a cup of warm milk, just tinged in color with coffee. In the days of my buoyant youth I said, 'of the color of the cheek of a brunette in Seville.' I had then never seen a brunette in Seville; but I have since, and I can testify that the description was good. Beef tea answers as well; a bowl of chowder quite as well as either. Indeed, good clam chowder is probably the form of nourishment which most quickly and easily comes to the restoration or refreshment of the brain of man.

"If this bowl of coffee, or chowder, or soup is counted as one meal, the working man who wishes to keep in order will have five meals a day, besides the morning cup of coffee, or of coffee colored with milk, which he has before breakfast. Breakfast is one; this extended lunch is another; dinner is the third, say at half-past two; tea is the fourth, at six or seven; and, what is too apt to be forgotten, a sufficient supper before bedtime is the fifth. This last may be as light as you please, but let it be sufficient,--a few oysters, a slice of hot toast, clam chowder again, or a bowl of soup. Never go to bed in any danger of being hungry. People are kept awake by hunger quite as much as by a bad conscience.

"Remembering that sleep is the essential force with which the whole scheme starts, decline tea or coffee within the last six hours before going to bed. If the women kind insist, you may have your milk and water at the tea-table, colored with tea; but the less the better.

"Avoid all mathematics or intricate study of any sort in the last six hours. This is the stuff dreams are made of, and hot heads, and the nuisances of waking hours.

"Keep your conscience clear. Remember that because the work of life is infinite you cannot do the whole of it in any limited period of time, and that, therefore, you may just as well leave off in one place as another.

"No work of any kind should be done in the hour after dinner. After any substantial meal, observe, you need all your vital force for the beginning of digestion. For my part, I always go to sleep after dinner and sleep for exactly an hour, if people will only stay away; and I am much more fond of the people who keep away from me at that time than I am of the people who visit me."

XIV.

A Humorist's Regimen.

Robert Barr (whose pseudonym, "Luke Sharp," is familiar to the readers of the Detroit Free Press) has written an article on "How a Literary Man Should Live," which may be cited in conclusion:--

"I am not," he says, "an advocate of early rising. I believe, however, that every literary man should have fixed hours for getting up. I am very firm with myself on that score. I make it a rule to rise every morning in winter between the hours of six and eleven, and in summer from half-past five until ten. A person is often tempted to sleep later than the limit I tie myself to, but a little resolution with a person's self at first will be amply repaid by the time thus gained, and the feeling one has of having conquered a tendency to indolence. I believe that a literary man can get all the sleep he needs between eight o'clock at night and eleven in the morning. I know, of course, that some eminent authorities disagree with me, but I am only stating my own experience in the matter, and don't propose to enter into any controversy about it.

"On rising I avoid all stimulating drinks, such as tea or coffee. They are apt to set the brain working, and I object to work, even in its most disguised forms. A simple glass of hot Scotch, say half a pint or so, serves to tide over the period between getting up and breakfast-time. Many literary men work before breakfast, but this I regard as a very dangerous habit. I try to avoid it, and so far have been reasonably successful. I rest until breakfast-time. This gives the person a zest for the morning meal.

"For breakfast the simplest food is the best. I begin with oyster stew, then some cold chicken, next a few small lamb chops and mashed potatoes, after that a good-sized beefsteak and fried potatoes, then a rasher of bacon with fried eggs (three), followed by a whitefish or two, the meal being completed with some light, wholesome pastry, mince pie for preference. Care should be taken to avoid tea or coffee, and I think a word of warning ought to go forth against milk. The devastation that milk has wrought among literary men is fearful to contemplate. They begin, thinking that if they find it is hurting them, they can break off, but too often before they awaken to their danger the habit has mastered them. I avoid anything at breakfast except a large tumbler of brandy, with a little soda water added to give it warmth and strength.

"No subject is of more importance to the literary aspirant than the dividing of the hours of work. I divide the hours just as minutely as I can, and then take as few of the particles as possible. I owe much of my success in life to the fact that I never allow work to interfere with the sacred time between breakfast and dinner. That is devoted to rest and thought. Much comfort can be realized during these hours by thinking what a stir you would make in the literary world if you could hire a man like Howells for five dollars a week to do your work for you. Such help, I find, is very difficult to obtain, and yet some people hold that the labor market is overcrowded. The great task of the forenoon should be preparation for the mid-day meal. The thorough enjoyment of this meal has much to do with a man's success in this life.

"Of course, I do not insist that a person should live like a hermit. Because he breakfasts frugally, that is no reason why he should not dine sumptuously. Some people dine at six and merely lunch at noon. Others have their principal meal in the middle of the day, and have a light supper. There is such merit in both these plans that I have adopted both. I take a big dinner and a light lunch at noon, and a heavy dinner and a simple supper in the evening. A person whose brain is constantly worried about how he can shove off his work on somebody else has to have a substantial diet. The bill of fare for dinner should include everything that abounds in the market--that the literary man can get trusted for.

"After a good rest when dinner is over, remain quiet until supper-time, so that the brain will not be too much agitated for the trials that come after that meal.

"I am a great believer in the old adage of 'early to bed.' We are apt to slight the wisdom of our forefathers; but they knew what they were about when they advised early hours. I always get to bed early,--say two or three in the morning. I do not believe in night work. It is rarely of a good quality. The brain is wearied with the exertions of the day and should not be overtaxed. Besides, the time can be put in with less irksomeness at the theatre, or in company with a lot of congenial companions who avoid the stimulating effects of tea, coffee, and milk. Tobacco, if used at all, should be sparingly indulged in. I never allow myself more than a dozen cigars a day; although, of course, I supplement this with a pipe.

"When do I do my literary work? Why, next day, of course."

THE END